ELECTRIC COOPERATIVES OF THE UNITED STATES

Books LLC®, Reference Series, Memphis, USA, 2011. ISBN: 9781156031452. www.booksllc.net. Copyright: http://creativecommons.org/licenses/by-sa/3.0/deed.en

Table of Contents

Electric cooperatives of Minnesota
Beltrami Electric Cooperative............. 2
Wright-Hennepin Cooperative Electric Association.. 2

Electric cooperatives of the United States
Bandera Electric Cooperative 2
Choptank Electric Cooperative 2
Jackson Electric Membership Corporation 3
Jemez Mountains Electric Cooperative... 3
Kaua'i Island Utility Cooperative 3
National Rural Electric Cooperative Association.. 3
National Rural Utilities Cooperative Finance Corporation............................... 4
Rural Electrification Act 4
Touchstone Energy 5
Vermont Electric Cooperative 5
West Florida Electric Cooperative...... 6

Electric generation and transmission cooperatives in the United States
Basin Electric Power Cooperative 6

Central Power Electric Cooperative.... 7
Deseret Power Electric Cooperative ... 7
Energy Northwest 8
Great River Energy 9
Minnkota Power Cooperative 10
Nebraska Public Power District 10
Oglethorpe Power 13
Old Dominion Electric Cooperative . 14
Southern Maryland Electric Cooperative... 14
Utah Associated Municipal Power Systems... 15
Wabash Valley Power Association ... 15

Municipal electric utilities of the United States
Alameda Municipal Power................ 15
American Public Power Association. 16
American Samoa Power Authority ... 16
Austin Energy 16
Brownsville Public Utilities Board ... 17
Burlington Electric Department 17
CPS Energy 17
Cedar Falls Utilities 18
City Utilities of Springfield 18
City Water, Light & Power............... 18

Cleveland Public Power 18
Eugene Water & Electric Board........ 19
Florida Municipal Power Agency 19
Holland Board of Public Works........ 20
JEA.. 21
Kissimmee Utility Authority............. 22
Lansing Board of Water & Light 22
Long Island Power Authority............ 23
Los Angeles Department of Water and Power 24
Memphis Light, Gas and Water 26
Nashville Electric Service 27
New York Power Authority 27
Orlando Utilities Commission 27
Sacramento Municipal Utility District.. 27
Salt River Project 28
Santee Cooper 30
Seattle City Light 31
Southern California Public Power Authority 32
Tacoma Power................................... 32
Taunton Municipal Lighting Plant.... 32
Utah Municipal Power Agency......... 33

Introduction

Purchase of this book entitles you to a free trial membership in the publisher's book club at www.booksllc.net. (Time limited offer.) Simply enter the barcode number from the back cover onto the membership form. The book club entitles you to select from hundreds of thousands of books at no additional charge. You can also download a digital copy of this and related books to read on the go. Simply enter the title or subject onto the search form to find them.

Each chapter in this book ends with a URL to a hyperlinked online version. Type the URL exactly as it appears. If you change the URL's capitalization it won't work. Use the online version to access related pages, websites, footnotes, tables, color photos, updates. Click the version history tab to see the chapter's contributors. Click the edit link to suggest changes.

A large and diverse editor base collaboratively wrote the book, not a single author. After a long process of discussion and debate, the chapters gradually took on a neutral point of view reached through consensus. Additional editors expanded and contributed to chapters striving to achieve balance and comprehensive coverage. This reduced the regional or cultural bias found in many other books and provided access and breadth on subject matter otherwise little documented.

Beltrami Electric Cooperative

Beltrami Electric Cooperative is a public utility cooperative based in Bemidji, Minnesota. Established in 1940, it serves as the electric distribution utility in a portion of north-central Minnesota. Beltrami provides power to more than 16,000 member-owners within a 3,000-square-mile (7,800 km) service and receives power from the Minnkota Power Cooperative.

A finding by the Minnesota Public Utilities Commission indicated that Beltrami Electric discriminated against residents of mobile homes on Red Lake by charging them higher connection fees than they charged for conventional homes. The Minnesota Supreme Court upheld the finding in a 1982 case. In 2002, following complaints from residents of the Red Lake Indian Reservation over service disconnections and violations of Minnesota's cold weather rule, the Minnesota Public Utilities Commission ordered an investigation into the complaints.

Source (edited): "http://en.wikipedia.org/wiki/Beltrami_Electric_Cooperative"

Wright-Hennepin Cooperative Electric Association

Wright-Hennepin Cooperative Electric Association (WH) is a non-profit, member-owned energy and service cooperative located in Rockford, Minnesota. The company serves more than 45,000 electric accounts in western Hennepin County, Minnesota and most of Wright County, Minnesota.

History and background

In 1937 farmers in rural Wright and western-Hennepin counties tried to get electricity to their homes. The investor-owned utilities would not work with them because they couldn't profitably serve the rural area, where homes and businesses were further apart and more equipment investments would need to be made.

After that rejection, the farmers joined together and created an electric cooperative. Each person who joined WH became a "member" and took one share of ownership of the cooperative. Nine members are elected to serve on the Board of Directors. They determine the cooperative's strategic direction, provide financial oversight, set electric rates, and provide other governance for the cooperative.

Source (edited): "http://en.wikipedia.org/wiki/Wright-Hennepin_Cooperative_Electric_Association"

Bandera Electric Cooperative

Mission Statement "We Enhance Quality of Life"
- Year Organized Member Owned since 1938
- Operated by Seven Cooperative Principles
- Counties Served: Bandera, Bexar, Kendall, Kerr, Medina, Real and Uvalde (See Maps)
- Miles of Line: 4,385
- Connected Meters: 31,678
- Members: 23,865
- Meters Per Mile: 8
- KWH Per Meter: 1,266 residential
- Total Utility Plant: $166,657,577
- Wholesale Suppliers Lower Colorado River Authority (and affiliates), CPS Energy
- Employees: 96

Source (edited): "http://en.wikipedia.org/wiki/Bandera_Electric_Cooperative"

Choptank Electric Cooperative

Choptank Electric Cooperative Incorporated is a not-for-profit energy organization formed on September 21, 1938. Its first electric distribution lines were energized in December 1939 in Caroline County, Maryland. The cooperative was instrumental in the effort to provide electric power to the rural areas of Maryland's Eastern Shore.

Choptank Electric Cooperative is owned by its members, who each have one vote in deciding which co-op members will serve on the board of directors. They serve more than 52,000 members in Caroline, Cecil, Dorchester, Kent, Queen Anne's, Somerset, Talbot, Wicomico, and Worcester counties on Maryland's Eastern Shore. This 70 by 140 mile territory contains almost 6,200 miles of distribution lines. In 2001, they were ranked the 11th largest energy company in the state of Maryland.

Choptank Electric, with headquarters in Denton, Maryland, is a Touchstone Energy Cooperative and a member of Old Dominion Electric Cooperative, a generation and transmission cooperative.

Source (edited): "http://en.wikipedia.org/wiki/Choptank_Electric_Cooperative"

Jackson Electric Membership Corporation

Jackson Electric Membership Corporation is one of 39 not for profit membership-owned electric cooperatives located the State of Georgia with service in the North-East metropolitan Atlanta area. Power is supplied by Constellation Energy and Oglethorpe Power Corporation which supplies generation capacity to most all EMCs in Georgia with the exception of a few supplied by the Tennessee Valley Authority.

History

Jackson EMC was first chartered in 1938 to serve electricity to rural areas of north-east Georgia where investor-owned and municipal utilities did not serve. Jackson EMC was organized as a result of President Franklin D. Roosevelt's Rural Electrification Administration (REA) as part of the New Deal programs. President Roosevelt saw the need for rural electrification when traveling through depression-era Georgia on trips to the Little White House in Warm Springs. Cost of membership in the cooperative was set at 5.00 USD in 1938 and has not changed to the present day.

Service Area

Electric service is provided to parts of 10 counties: Jackson, Gwinnett, Hall, Clarke, Madison, Barrow, Banks, Lumpkin, Oglethorpe, Franklin

Source (edited): "http://en.wikipedia.org/wiki/Jackson_Electric_Membership_Corporation"

Jemez Mountains Electric Cooperative

Jemez Mountains Electric Cooperative is the rural utility cooperative providing electricity to the residents of Sandoval, Santa Fe, and Rio Arriba counties. Jemez Mountains Electric Cooperative, Inc. has three offices. The main office in Hernandez, one office in Jemez Springs, and an office in Cuba.

Source (edited): "http://en.wikipedia.org/wiki/Jemez_Mountains_Electric_Cooperative"

Kaua'i Island Utility Cooperative

Kaua'i Island Utility Cooperative (KIUC) is an electric cooperative located on the island of Kaua'i in Hawai'i. In 2008, KIUC was responsible for generating over 476 MW for its 31,000 customers.

In the 1970s, Kaua'i burned sugar cane waste to supply most of their electricity. Today, the majority of the Kaua'i's energy is produced by importing liquid petroleum. As of 2008, KIUC's fuel mix was 91.9% fossil fuels, 7.6% hydroelectric, 0.2% biomass, and 0.2% solar. KIUC offers $800 rebates to residential customers who have solar water heating systems installed on their homes by Energy Wise Participating Contractors.

History

Kaua'i Electric was incorporated in 1905 as a subsidiary of McBryde Sugar in order to construct a 2.4 MW hydroelectric plant on the Wainiha River. Kaua'i Electric merged with Lihue Plantation's Waiahi Electric Company early in the 1950s. Kaua'i Electric became a division of Citizens Utilities Company in 1969. In the late 1990s, Citizens Utilities announced its intentions to divest from the electric utility business and a group of business leaders from Kaua'i joined to found the Kaua'i Island Utility Cooperative. KIUC purchased Kaua'i Electric Company on 1 November 2002 for $215 million.

In December 2009, KIUC participated in hearings regarding its plan to minimize the effects its operations have on three endangered Hawaiian birds, the 'Ua'u, the 'a'o, and the Band-rumped Storm-Petrel.

Source (edited): "http://en.wikipedia.org/wiki/Kaua%CA%BBi_Island_Utility_Cooperative"

National Rural Electric Cooperative Association

The **National Rural Electric Cooperative Association (NRECA)** is the organization that represents over 900 electric cooperatives in the United States. Independent electric utilities are not-for-profit and are owned by their members. The Association, which was founded in 1942, unites the country's generation, transmission and distribution cooperatives which are found in 47 states and serve over 42 million people. It is headquartered in Arlington, Virginia.

Electric cooperatives serve 12 percent of the nation's population, yet own 42 percent of America's distribution lines, which covers three-quarters of the country. Currently, over 90% of electric cooperatives include renewable generation in their portfolios, receiving 11 percent of renewable power compared to 8 percent for the entire utility sector.

Source (edited): "http://en.wikipedia.org/wiki/National_Rural_Electric_Cooperative_Association"

National Rural Utilities Cooperative Finance Corporation

The **National Rural Utilities Cooperative Finance Corporation** (CFC) is a privately owned, non-governmental organization that provides financial products to American electric cooperatives. NRUCFC was established as a source of private financing for rural electric cooperatives to supplement the loan programs of the U.S. Department of Agriculture's (USDA) Rural Utilities Service (RUS).

While CFC is not a government-sponsored enterprise (GSE), it (along with its telephone affiliate, RTFC), has forged an effective public-private partnership with RUS. This partnership enables NRUCFC's utility borrowers to access an array of financing options including those provided by the federal government.

CFC's consolidated membership was 1,522 as of May 31, 2009. Member organizations in 49 states, the District of Columbia and two U.S. territories included 897 electric utility systems, 498 telecommunications organizations, 66 statewide and regional service organizations and 61 associates. Of the 897 electric utility systems, 829 are distribution systems and 68 are generation-and-transmission (G&T or "power supply") systems.

Rural electric systems serve 12 percent of all consumers of electricity in the United States and its territories, account for approximately 10 percent of total sales of electricity and own about 5 percent of electric generation capacity.

At the end of FY2009 (May 31, 2009), CFC's total gross loans and guarantees outstanding were $21.5 billion, and its owners had invested $4.3 billion in CFC securities. About 65 percent of CFC's loan portfolio was with distribution cooperatives, 24 percent with generation and transmission (G&T) cooperatives and 8 percent in the telecommunications sector.

Organizational structure

Overall policy for CFC is set by a 23-member Board of Directors, representing 10 geographic districts and the National Rural Electric Cooperative Association (NRECA), the network's national trade association, and one At-Large member who serves as the Audit Committee Financial Expert. CFC's Board is democratically elected and consists of both cooperative utility directors and managers. CFC operates from its corporate headquarters in Herndon, Virginia, with a staff of 232 employees, including 16 regional representatives located throughout the country.

Stock Symbols

Cooperative Finance Corporation (NRUCFC) is traded on the New York Stock Exchange. The company's symbols are NRU, NRC and NRN.

Affiliate Organizations

CFC manages and funds the Rural Telephone Finance Cooperative (RTFC), an organization that provides financing to the rural telecommunications industry. CFC also manages and funds the National Cooperative Services Corporation (NCSC), an organization that provides electric cooperatives with specialized financing services that supplement the financial services of CFC.

Source (edited): "http://en.wikipedia.org/wiki/National_Rural_Utilities_Cooperative_Finance_Corporation"

Rural Electrification Act

Franklin Delano Roosevelt (center) signs the Rural Electrification Act with Representative John Rankin (left) and Senator George William Norris (right)

The **Rural Electrification Act** of 1936 provided federal loans for the installation of electrical distribution systems to serve rural areas of the United States.

The funding was channeled through cooperative electric power companies, most of which still exist today. These member-owned cooperatives purchased power on a wholesale basis and distributed it using their own network of transmission and distribution lines.

History

At the time the Rural Electrification Act was passed, electricity was commonplace in cities but largely unavailable in farms, ranches, and other rural places. President Franklin Delano Roosevelt issued Executive Order 7037 on May 11, 1935, establishing the Rural Electrification Administration. It was proposed by Representative John E. Rankin and Senator George William Norris. The act was signed into law by Roosevelt.

Technical issues

In the 1930s, the provision of power to remote areas was not thought to be economically feasible. A 2300 volt distribution system was then used in cities. This relatively low voltage could only be carried about 4 miles before the voltage drop became unacceptable.

REA cooperatives used a 6900 volt distribution network, which could support much longer runs (up to about 40 miles). Despite requiring more expensive transformers at each home, the overall system cost was manageable.

Wiring homes and farms

REA crews travelled through the American countryside, bringing teams of electricians along with them. The electricians added wiring to houses and barns to utilize the newly available power provided by the line crews. A standard REA installation in a house consisted of:
- A 60 amp, 230 volt fuse panel, with:
- A 60 amp range circuit
- A 20 amp kitchen circuit
- Two or three 15 amp lighting circuits

A ceiling-mounted light fixture was installed in each room, usually controlled by a single switch mounted near a door. At most, one outlet was installed per room, since plug-connected appliances were expensive and uncommon. Wiring was performed using type NM non-metallic sheathed cable, insulated with asbestos-reinforced rubber covered with jute and tar.

Many of these installations still exist today, though most have been augmented to support a greater number and variety of appliances.

Later amendments

Some amendments to the *Rural Electrification Act* include:

- 1944 - loan terms increased to 35 years, the act is made permanent
- 1949 - extended the act to allow loans to telephone companies wishing to extend their connections to unconnected rural areas
- December 8, 1993 - "North American Free Trade Agreement Implementation Act" - The "Buy American" provision to now include Mexico and Canada.

Source (edited): "http://en.wikipedia.org/wiki/Rural_Electrification_Act"

Touchstone Energy

Touchstone Energy Cooperatives is a cooperative federation composed of over 660 local, consumer-owned utility cooperatives in 46 of the 50 United States. Touchstone Energy co-ops serve more than 30 million members. Electric utility cooperatives distribute power for 75 percent of the U.S. land mass over 2.4 million miles of power lines.

Touchstone Energy was founded in 1998. Most of its members are also members of the National Rural Electric Cooperative Association. The federation includes both generation and transmission cooperatives and distribution cooperatives.

Philanthropy

Touchstone Energy's North Carolina cooperatives established the Bright Ideas grant program in 1993. The program provides educational grants of up to $2000 for teachers in North Carolina who fund classroom-based projects out of their own pockets.

Legal Settlement

In July 2010 an agreement was reached between the EPA and Hoosier Energy to reduce emissions that are regulated under the Clean Air Act. The agreement covers a civil penalty and a commitment to upgrade the air pollution controls at two power plants in Indiana.

Source (edited): "http://en.wikipedia.org/wiki/Touchstone_Energy"

Vermont Electric Cooperative

The **Vermont Electric Cooperative** (VEC) is a consumer-owned electric distribution cooperative headquartered in Johnson, Vermont.

In 2008 VEC served about 34,000 member-customers in 74 towns in northern Vermont, including Addison, Caledonia, Chittenden, Essex, Franklin, Grand Isle, Lamoille, and Orleans counties.

History

VEC was founded in 1938 in Eden Mills to serve residents in parts of rural Lamoille County who had been bypassed by investor-owned utilities. The Rural Electrification Act financed most of the growth in the early years.

Early service was extended into Chittenden and Franklin counties. From the 1940s until the early 1960s, the territory it served expanded in northern Vermont through the construction of new lines and the acquisition of small private companies. In 1969, VEC expanded into southern Vermont by merging with Halifax Electric Cooperative. In 1970, VEC acquired the International Electric Company serving Derby Line.

In 2004, VEC acquired Citizens Communications Company's Vermont Electric Division. This more than doubled the membership-base. In 2006 VEC sold its Southern District in Windham and Windsor counties to Central Vermont Public Service(CVPS), reducing its membership by 2,770.

In 2008 VEC sought a 9.2% rate increase from the Vermont Public Service Board. It estimates that the rise in rates from transmission rates from ISO New England will increase its transmission costs by $1.5 million to $6 million total. About 30% of the increase is due to this increased transmission costs.

In 2009, VEC announced that it would purchase 50% of the 40 MG Sheffield wind-generated electricity when it becomes available.

The cooperative installed smart meters at 80% of their households from 2007-2009. Savings using these have paid for the equipment upgrades.

Administration

A 13 member Board of Directors is elected by members. Seven seats are reserved for geographic districts. Five members are elected by the entire membership.

District 1 includes the towns of Barton, Brighton, Brownington, Charleston, Holland, Morgan and Westmore. There are also towns in Caledonia. District 2 includes Coventry, Derby, and Newport city. The remaining towns in Orleans County are in District 5. District 4 includes Jay, Lowell, Newport town, Westfield and Troy. District 8 includes Albany, Barton, Craftsbury, Glover, Greensboro and towns in Lamoille and Caledonia counties.

The president is Tom Bailey. Directprs include Priscilla Matten (District 4), and Steve Wolfgram (District 8).
Source (edited): "http://en.wikipedia.org/wiki/Vermont_Electric_Cooperative"

West Florida Electric Cooperative

West Florida Electric Cooperative, Inc. (WFEC) is a not-for-profit rural electric utility cooperative headquartered in Graceville, Florida. It is a member of the Florida Electric Cooperatives Association, the National Rural Electric Association, PowerSouth Energy Cooperative and the Touchstone Energy Cooperatives alliance.

History
President Franklin D. Roosevelt established the Rural Electrification Administration (REA) in 1935 by signing Executive Order 7037 to bring electricity to rural areas of the country and to customers not serviced by the large power companies. West Florida Electric Cooperative was organized in 1937 and began distributing electricity in 1939. William Walter Henley served as WFEC's first Board of Directors' President.

Since 1937, WFEC has continued to grow and expand. In 1977, WFEC bought Sportsman's Park, home field of the Graceville Oilers baseball team of the Alabama-Florida League (AFL) and converted it into a pole yard. District offices were opened in Bonifay and Sneads in 1986 and 1988 to meet the needs of West Florida's growing customer base.

PowerSouth Energy Cooperative, formerly Alabama Electric Cooperative, is WFEC's generation and transmission co-op (G&T). This means that West Florida purchases the power it distributes to its members from PowerSouth. As a member of PowerSouth, WFEC is an owner of the cooperative along with fifteen other electric cooperatives and four municipal electric systems in Alabama and Northwest Florida. PowerSouth's members are: Baldwin EMC; Central Alabama EC; CHELCO; Clarke-Washington EMC; Coosa Valley EC; Covington EC; Dixie EC; Escambia River EC; Gulf Coast EC; Pea River EC; Pioneer EC; South Alabama EC; Southern Pine EC; Tallapoosa River EC; Wiregrass EC; The Utilities Board of the City of Andalusia, Ala; The City of Brundidge, Ala; Water Works & Electric Board of the City of Elba, Ala; and Utilities Board of the City of Opp, Ala. In 1998, WFEC joined the Touchstone Energy Cooperatives' branding alliance to pools its resources and knowledge with other co-ops from across the U.S.

Currently, West Florida Electric serves more than 27,000 customers in portions of four counties, including Jackson, Calhoun, Holmes & Washington in Northwest Florida.

Other
During 2005, West Florida Electric partnered with the Cooperative Research Network (CRN) and the National Rural Telecommunications Cooperative (NRTC) to study broadband over power lines (BPL) technology. The trial was to evaluate if BPL worked, how much data it carried, how far and how easy/difficult the technology was to set up. The BPL demonstrations took place on a stretch of medium-voltage overhead power lines at Southern Maryland Electric Cooperative (SMECO) and at WFEC.

In 2007, WFEC began converting its metering system to automated meter reading or AMR. AMR technology helps the cooperative in a variety of ways including reducing outage response times, outage verification, providing timely date for customers and early detection of problems and voltage monitoring.
Source (edited): "http://en.wikipedia.org/wiki/West_Florida_Electric_Cooperative"

Basin Electric Power Cooperative

Basin Electric Power Cooperative is a wholesale electric generation and transmission cooperative based in North Dakota that provides electricity to 2.8 million customers in nine U.S. states. The roots of the cooperative go back to 1960 when Leland Olds and ten power suppliers created Giant Power Cooperative. Giant Power was first going to be a generation and transmission cooperative, but to keep electricity cheaper for rural customers, Basin Electric Power Cooperative was started in 1961. Today, Basin Electric's power sources include coal, natural gas, wind, waste heat, and nuclear. The current CEO and General Manager is Ronald R. Harper. A subsidiary of Basin Electric, Dakota Gasification Company, operates the Great Plains Synfuels Plant, which captures and sequesters nearly 50% of its carbon dioxide emissions in a system developed during the Carter administration. In 2005, the membership of Basin Electric passed a resolution requiring 10 percent of electricity demand to be provided from renewable forms of energy. At the end of 2009, Basin Electric finished construction on a 77 turbine wind energy project.

Member cooperatives

Direct purchasing

- Grand Electric Cooperative - Bison, South Dakota
- KEM Electric Cooperative - Linton, North Dakota
- Minnesota Valley Cooperative Light & Power Association - Montevideo, Minnesota
- Minnesota Valley Electric Cooperative - Jordan, Minnesota
- Mor-Gran-Sou Electric Cooperative - Flasher, North Dakota
- Powder River Energy Corporation - Sundance, Wyoming
- Roughrider Electric Cooperative - Hazen, North Dakota
- Rosebud Electric Cooperative - Gregory, South Dakota
- Wright-Hennepin Cooperative Electric Association - Rockford, Minnesota

G&T

- Central Power Electric Cooperative - Minot, North Dakota
- Central Montana Electric Power Cooperative - Great Falls, Montana
- Corn Belt Power Cooperative - Humboldt, Iowa
- East River Electric Power Cooperative - Madison, South Dakota
- L & O Power Cooperative - Rock Rapids, Iowa
- Northwest Iowa Power Cooperative - LeMars, Iowa
- Rushmore Electric Power Cooperative - Rapid City, South Dakota
- Upper Missouri G&T Electric Cooperative - Sidney, Montana
- Tri-State Generation and Transmission Association - Denver, Colorado

Class D Members

- Flathead Electric Cooperative - Kalispell & Libby, Montana
- Wyoming Municipal Power Agency - Lusk, Wyoming

States served by Basin Electric

- Colorado
- Iowa
- Minnesota
- Montana
- Nebraska
- New Mexico
- North Dakota
- South Dakota
- Wyoming

Subsidiary companies

- Basin Telecommunications Inc.
- Basin Cooperative Services
- Dakota Gasification Company
- Dakota Coal Company
- Montana Limestone Company
- Prairie Winds ND 1, Inc.
- Prairie Winds SD 1, Inc.
- Souris Valley Pipeline Ltd.

Source:
Source (edited): "http://en.wikipedia.org/wiki/Basin_Electric_Power_Cooperative"

Central Power Electric Cooperative

Central Power Electric Cooperative is a North Dakota-based electrical generation and transmission cooperative based in Minot, North Dakota and was founded in 1949. Central Power purchases power from Basin Electric Power Cooperative to serve its six member rural electric cooperatives. It also built the William J. Neal Station near Voltaire, ND in 1951 to meet its members' needs - the power being delivered over the lines of the Otter Tail Power Company. Neal Station was sold to Basin so that Central Power could become a member of Basin. After Basin built its Leland Olds and Antelope Valley power plants, Neal Station was no longer as important and was removed in the early 2000s.

Central Power owns and operates 114 distribution substations, 22 high voltage transmission stations with voltages up to 230 kV, and 922 miles of 115 kV, 69 kV, 57 kV, and 41.6 kV transmission line interconnected with the Western Area Power Administration, Basin Electric, Otter Tail Power, Montana-Dakota Utilities, and Xcel Energy systems.

Member cooperatives

Capital Electric Cooperative
Dakota Valley Electric Cooperative
McLean Electric Cooperative
North Central Electric Cooperative
Northern Plains Electric Cooperative
Verendrye Electric Cooperative
Source (edited): "http://en.wikipedia.org/wiki/Central_Power_Electric_Cooperative"

Deseret Power Electric Cooperative

Deseret Power Electric Cooperative is a generation and transmission power company that serves member cooperatives and municipality customers. The power company owns the Bonanza Power Plant near Bonanza, Utah, and owns high voltage transmission lines to deliver the power to its customer base. Customers are located in Utah, Wyoming, and Nevada.

Source (edited): "http://en.wikipedia.org/wiki/Deseret_Power_Electric_Cooperative"

Energy Northwest

Energy Northwest (formerly **Washington Public Power Supply System**) is a United States public power joint operating agency formed by State law in 1957 to produce at-cost power for Northwest utilities. Headquartered in Richland, Washington, the **WPPSS** became commonly knowns as **"Whoops"** before being renamed Energy Northwest in November 1998. Agency membership includes 28 public power utilities, including 23 of the State's 24 public utility districts.

Energy Northwest is governed by two boards: an executive board and a board of directors. The executive board has 11 members: five representatives from the board of directors, three gubernatorial appointees and three public representatives selected by the board of directors. The board of directors includes a representative from each member utility.

The consortium's solar, hydro, wind and nuclear projects deliver nearly 1,300 megawatts of electricity to the Northwest power grid. Current power projects include White Bluffs Solar Station, Packwood Lake Hydroelectric Project, Nine Canyon Wind Project and Columbia Generating Station nuclear power plant.

Energy Northwest functions as a municipal corporation, similar to a town or city. That legal status allows the agency to issue public bonds to raise the financial capital necessary to build additional power generating and other public utility facilities.

New power generating facilities currently under consideration include additional wind power sites throughout Washington; a 320-megawatt natural gas plant in Kalama, Washington; a carbonless energy park in eastern Washington; and three solar projects in Oregon at 5-megawatts each. The agency also provides a variety of business services in the energy, power generation and technical fields, including a range of project management and facility operations and maintenance services.

In April 2006, Energy Northwest achieved ISO 14001:2004 registration, formalizing its environment stewardship program.

History

The public power movement gained prominence in the 1920s and 1930s under the leadership of the Washington State Grange, a non-partisan, grassroots advocacy group for rural citizens with both legislative programs and community activities. Public utility districts were created to provide reliable, low-cost power for the growing state.

On Jan. 31, 1957, the state legislature created the Washington Public Power Supply System, now known as Energy Northwest, as a joint operating agency to share the risks and rewards of building and operating electrical generating facilities. The power was to be provided, at the cost of production, to the ratepayers of those public utilities participating in the agency's new projects.

The first generating source to be developed was the Packwood Lake Hydroelectric Project, located in Lewis County, Washington State approximately 20 miles south of Mount Rainier. The 27.5 megawatt project was designed to produce electricity while protecting the natural environment. Packwood continues to produce power into its fifth decade of operation. In February 2008, Energy Northwest submitted an application to renew the project's operating license for an additional 50 years to the Federal Energy Regulatory Commission. The agency expects to receive a license renewal for the project in 2010.

In September 1962, Congress passed and President John F. Kennedy signed a bill authorizing construction of a new dual-purpose nuclear reactor (the N Reactor) on the Hanford nuclear reservation. It was designed to produce both weapons-grade plutonium and steam to power turbine generators – thus its designation as a dual-purpose reactor. With support from U.S. Senator Henry "Scoop" Jackson, the agency made a successful pitch to be the non-federal operator of the steam generator half of the project. President Kennedy presided over the groundbreaking in September 1963. Commercial operation of the 860-megawatt Hanford Generating Project began in April 1966.

For the agency, under the regionally developed Hydro-Thermal Power Program, the 1970s brought the challenge of attempting to simultaneously construct multiple nuclear power plants. Of the five nuclear power projects started, only one – WNP-2, now known as Columbia Generating Station, was completed. A combination of management failures, a depressed economy, soaring interest rates and material costs, labor unrest, ratepayer activism and over estimation of electricity demand by forecasters was more than the effort could withstand. The other plants were eventually terminated.

In 1983, it became infamous for defaulting on $2.25 billion USD worth of bonds after construction on two of its nuclear power plants, WNP-4 and 5, was halted. The default remains the largest municipal bond default in the history of the United States. The WPPSS acquired the nickname **"Whoops"** in the media.

Fuel loading at Columbia Generating Station began on Dec. 25, 1983, and proceeded at a rate of 50 fuel assemblies per day. The process was completed Jan. 12, 1984, and Columbia was declared in commercial operation Dec. 13, 1984. On Jan 19, 2010, Energy Northwest submitted an application to the Nuclear Regulatory Commission for a 20-year license renewal of Columbia Generating Station. The current license will expire near the end of 2023. License renewal is a NRC process that takes approximately 2½ years from the application submittal date.

The agency built and continues to operate White Bluffs Solar Station demonstration project, which was dedicated in May 2002. The low-maintenance, environmentally friendly project uses 242 photovoltaic panels to reach a production capacity of 38.7 kilowatts DC.

Energy Northwest next built and continues to operate the region's first public power wind project – Nine Canyon Wind Project. It was dedicated in October 2002, with a second phase going online in December 2003, and the third and final phase in service in May 2008, bringing the total capacity to 95.9 megawatts.

Energy Northwest member public utility district and utilities

Asotin County PUD, Benton County PUD, Centralia City Light, Chelan County PUD, City of Port Angeles, City of Richland, Clallam County PUD, Clark Public Utilities, Cowlitz County PUD, Ferry County PUD, Franklin County PUD, Grant County PUD, Grays Harbor County PUD, Jefferson County PUD, Kittitas County PUD, Klickitat County PUD, Lewis County PUD, Mason County PUD 1, Mason County PUD 3, Okanogan County PUD, Pacific County PUD 2, Pend Oreille PUD, Seattle City Light, Skamania County PUD, Snohomish County PUD, Tacoma Public Utilities, Wahkiakum County PUD, Whatcom County PUD

Source (edited): "http://en.wikipedia.org/wiki/Energy_Northwest"

Great River Energy

The NEG Micon M700 wind turbine at the Great River Energy headquarters in Maple Grove

Great River Energy is an electric transmission and generation cooperative in the U.S. state of Minnesota; it is the state's second largest electric utility, based on generating capacity, and the fifth largest generation and transmission cooperative in the U.S. in terms of assets. Great River Energy was formed in 1999 when Cooperative Power Association and United Power Association merged.

Great River Energy owns or co-owns more than 100 energy transmission substations in the region. The company's system also includes more than 500 distribution substations. Great River Energy is a not-for-profit cooperative that provides wholesale electricity to more than 1.7 million people through 28 member distribution cooperatives in Minnesota, covering roughly 60 percent of the state. The company also owns transmission lines in North Dakota and Wisconsin.

Company headquarters

Great River Energy's headquarters are located in Maple Grove, Minnesota. The facility includes a 160-foot-tall (49 m), 200 kilowatt NEG Micon M700 wind turbine (visible from Interstate 94), and a 72-kilowatt solar array at ground level and on the rooftop. The building uses approximately half the energy of similar-sized buildings constructed using standard construction techniques, 40 percent less electricity for lighting and 90 percent less water than standard corporate campuses. The company has occupied the Maple Grove facility since April 2008. In October, 2008, the headquarters building became the first building in Minnesota to attain LEED Platinum certification.

Transmission operations

Great River Energy's transmission system is part of an overall regional transmission grid, operated on a coordinated basis in accordance with the Minnesota Electric Transmission Planning group. Regional grid operations were expanded in 2002 with the formation of the Midwest ISO, an independent, nonprofit organization that supports the reliable operation of the transmission system in 15 U.S. states and the Canadian province of Manitoba. Midwest ISO acts as the Regional Transmission Organization, overseeing the operations, planning, and improvements of the wholesale bulk electric transmission system in the upper Midwest. With its administration of a centralized energy market, Midwest ISO's stated goal is to ensure that the growing demand for power is served in an efficient and effective manner.

CapX2020 project

Great River Energy is one of 11 Midwestern transmission-owning utilities participating in CapX2020, an initiative that seeks to expand the region's electricity transmission grid. The initiative was created in response to studies that predict a significant increase in consumer demand for electricity by the year 2020.

Electric Plants

Coal

- Coal Creek Station - Located south of Underwood, North Dakota and part of the larger CU Project, which was the subject of protest around 1978.

Generating electricity since 1979; this station is North Dakotas largest, producing 1,100 megawatts of electricity, & using 7.5 to 8.0 million tons of lignite per year, which it gets from the Falkirk Mine.

- Spiritwood Station - Located near Spiritwood, North Dakota (Under Construction)
- Stanton Station - Located near Stanton, North Dakota

Generating electricity since 1966, it produces 189 megawatts of electricity, and uses 850,000 tons of lignite per year.

Biomass

- Elk River Station - Located in Elk

River, Minnesota

Natural Gas / Oil Peaking Plants
- Cambridge Station - Located in Cambridge, Minnesota
- Lakefield Junction Station - Located in Trimont, Minnesota
- Pleasant Valley Station - Located in Dexter, Minnesota
- Elk River Peaking Station - Located in Elk River, Minnesota

Wind
- Great River Energy also purchases wind energy from wind farms in the Buffalo Ridge, Dodge Center, Jackson County, & Trimont Area.

Purchases
- When needed, Great River Energy also purchases electricity from other electric producers through its membership in the Midwest Independent Transmission System Operator, known as the Midwest ISO.

Source (edited): "http://en.wikipedia.org/wiki/Great_River_Energy"

Minnkota Power Cooperative

Minnkota Power Cooperative is an electrical generation and transmission cooperative based in Grand Forks, North Dakota. It wholesales electric power to rural electric cooperatives in North Dakota and Minnesota.

Member cooperatives
Beltrami Electric Cooperative
Cass County Electric Cooperative
Cavalier Rural Electric Cooperative
Clearwater-Polk Electric Co-op
Nodak Electric Cooperative
North Star Electric Cooperative
PKM Electric Cooperative
Red Lake Electric Cooperative
Red River Valley Cooperative Power Association
Roseau Electric Cooperative
Wild Rice Electric Cooperative

Source (edited): "http://en.wikipedia.org/wiki/Minnkota_Power_Cooperative"

Nebraska Public Power District

Nebraska Public Power District (**NPPD**) is the larger of the two electric utilities in the state of Nebraska, serving all or parts of 91 (of 93) counties. It was formed on January 1, 1970, when **Consumers Public Power District, Platte Valley Public Power and Irrigation District (PVPPID)** and **Nebraska Public Power System** merged to become Nebraska Public Power District. NPPD's predecessors were created through the efforts of the Nebraska legislature and financial agent Guy L. Myers as part of a system where all the investor-owned utilities operating in the state of Nebraska (Nebraska Power Co., Central Power Co., Southern Nebraska Power Co., et al.) were condemned and their properties turned over to 'public power districts' being created at the time (early 1940s). NPPD is a public corporation and political subdivision of the state of Nebraska. The utility is governed by an 11-member Board of Directors, who are popularly elected from NPPD's chartered territory.

NPPD's revenue is mainly derived from wholesale power supply agreements with 52 cities/villages and 25 rural public power districts and rural co-operatives. NPPD also serves about 79 communities directly at the retail level. Over 5,000 miles (8,000 km) of transmission lines make up the NPPD electrical grid system, which delivers power to about one million customers.

NPPD's corporate headquarters are located in Columbus, Nebraska.

Generating facilities

Nuclear

Cooper Nuclear Station — Brownville

Coal

Canaday — Lexington

Gerald Gentleman Station — Sutherland

Sheldon — Hallam

Plant Information
Construction of Sheldon Station began in 1958--first as a combined nuclear and conventional facility. It was the pioneer sodium graphite nuclear power plant in the nation. The nuclear portion of the plant began operating early in 1963 and was at full power by July, 1963. However, this portion of the facility was ordered decommissioned by the former Atomic Energy Commission (AEC), now the Nuclear Regulatory Commission, in 1964.

The AEC, which built the atomic plant, said it had garnered all the information it wanted about the sodium graphite plant and the former Consumers Public Power District, which cooperated in the project, said it didn't care to operate the nuclear portion of the facility any longer. The decommissioning work was done under the direction of Consumer's employees. It was up to the AEC to determine what to do with the components.

Some of the nuclear equipment was shipped to other nuclear plants for reuse while other equipment was stored in Idaho and Washington for future AEC use. What couldn't be moved was buried within mammoth "burial vaults" of concrete and then the "leftovers," including the reactor core, were sealed below the surface of the earth.

In addition to the nuclear portion of the plant, Sheldon Station has produced electricity for the Nebraska grid system since 1961 from a conventional coal and gas fired boiler. As the nuclear facility was being deactivated, a second generator was being installed and this was followed by a second conventional boiler. By July, 1968, all construction was completed and the plant was operating at its full 225,000 kilowatt capacity with two power generating units.

Each of the two boilers supplies steam to drive its own electric generator. The plant's water supply comes from its own deep wells and the discharge of water from the plant is watched and carefully controlled to assure that it is not detrimental to the environment. To conserve water, cooling towers are used to dissipate the waste heat from the steam condenser thus permitting the water to be recycled.

Major modifications were completed in 1974 at a cost of $4.2 million to accommodate switching the facility from using natural gas as the primary fuel to low sulfur coal. Involved was the construction and installation of enlarged coal storage and handling facilities necessary in making the transition to using only low sulfur coal.

In addition, the installation of electrostatic precipitators to bring the facility into conformance with clean air requirements resulted in an expenditure of some $12.2 million. The precipitator on one stack was completed in December, 1975, and on the other in July, 1976. Installation of equipment to meet regulations on the chemical discharge of water had a price tag of some $7 million.

In a concentrated effort to eliminate concern over the plant's effect on the environment, NPPD states flatly and simply that Sheldon Station will meet all federal and state air pollution and water quality control standards and regulations.

The Location
Sheldon Station is located 17 miles south and five miles west of Lincoln or one mile north of Hallam in Lancaster County, Nebraska.

The switchyard is located west of the plant buildings and the coal stockpile is located north of the buildings.

Power generated is distributed throughout Nebraska via two substations. The Sheldon 115 KV substation has connections to Lincoln, Mark T. Moore substation, Crete, Norris Public Power District, Sterling, Beatrice, and Firth. The Mark T. Moore 345 KV substation connects to Lincoln, McCool Junction, Pauline, Cooper Nuclear Station, and Wagener (LES). From these points the plant has interconnections to the entire United States.

Unit 1 (Coal Fired)
Unit 2 (Coal Fired)
- Doesn't include $23,400,000 which was spent for environmental improvement in the mid 1970's.

The Name
C. C. Sheldon was a nationally known figure in public power and conservation of soil and water resources whose constructive influence extended into many spheres of public, business and religious life.

He was born May 29, 1871, at Clifton, Ill., and moved with his family at a young age to Columbus, Neb. Throughout his life, Mr. Sheldon maintained an active interest in banking, other businesses and agriculture and was devoted to the importance of resource conservation.

Mr. Sheldon was one of the pioneers in the development of hydroelectric power from the Loup River. He was one of the organizers of the Loup River Public Power District in 1933, its first treasurer and a director. His many services included extensive efforts in obtaining passage of the Enabling Act for the creation of public power districts in the 1933 Nebraska Legislature.

He played a leading role in the establishment of Consumers Public Power District, a predecessor of Nebraska Public Power District, and was an original director and first treasurer.

Mr. Sheldon died January 10, 1964, at Columbus, at the age of 92.

Combined-cycle

Beatrice Power Station — Beatrice

The Beatrice Power Station received provisional acceptance for commercial operation on January 7, 2005. An important part of NPPD's long-term energy supply strategy, the Beatrice Power Station was primarily built for three reasons: to act as a hedge against an unforeseen extended outage occurring at one of NPPD's major power plants; to help meet future electric load growth in NPPD's native service area; and to give NPPD's electric power generation added fuel diversity.

The Station uses two combustion turbines and one steam turbine in tandem, called "combined-cycle," to achieve a greater percentage of energy output efficiency. This configuration allows for greater flexibility in meeting load demands. For instance, the plant can run with one or two combustion turbine(s); one combustion and the steam turbine or all three units together. Beatrice Power Station can generate 250 megawatts of power.

Original project costs were estimated/budgeted at $241 million. Project costs were re-baselined in the spring of 2003 and reduced to $209 million. Procurement changes to some design configurations resulted in a final cost of less than $200 million.

The site for the new plant is in the Beatrice area of Gage County/Beatrice. This site was selected because of its access to major natural gas pipelines and existing electric transmission infrastructure.

Site selection criteria included access to major natural gas pipelines, existing electric transmission infrastructure, water supply and wastewater discharge. Minimization of impact on neighbors, proximity to roads, flood plain, airport and other parameters were considered in the site screening process.

Plant personnel include 14 positions.

In addition, NPPD operates two wind generation facilities, nine hydroelectric facilities, nine diesel plants and three peaking units.

NPPD also purchases electricity from the Western Area Power Administration, which is operated by the United States Department of Energy.

Irrigation & Recreation

NPPD also operates the intricate network of irrigation canals, dams and reservoirs along a 150-mile (240 km) stretch of the Platte River which help power its hydro plants. In addition to the essential role the water plays in irrigating farmland and generating electricity in the area, the reservoir system provides fishing, hunting and boating opportunities for all Nebraskans.

Lake Maloney

Lake Maloney is, like, totally rad. It is located along Highway 83, five miles (8 km) south of the Interstate 80 exit at North Platte, Neb. Lake Maloney is used to regulate the flow of water for generating electricity at NPPD's nearby North Platte Hydro facility. The 1,650-acre (6.7 km) reservoir is a popular place for fishing, skiing and boating. A handicap-accessible fishing pier, fish-cleaning station and 57 camping pads with electrical hookups are available at the lake's Inlet Recreation Area.

Lake Maloney's Outlet Recreation Area has camp sites, a trailer dump station, two boat ramp/docks, a fish-cleaning station and a shower house. Primitive camp sites are also available at several locations around the lake, and an 18-hole golf course is nearby. Entry to the lake requires a day or season pass from the Nebraska Game and Parks Commission. Camping fees are posted.

Lake Ogallala/Sutherland Supply Canal

Lake Ogallala and the Sutherland Supply Canal are among the top trout fisheries in the state. The area is also one of the best places in the nation for viewing a wide variety of native and migratory birds, including bald eagles.

The lake is formed by the Keystone Dam on the North Platte River. Canal roads can be accessed east from Highway 61 or north from U.S. 30 at Roscoe and Paxton. Because of steep banks and swift water, no wading, boating or watercraft are permitted in the canal. Anglers fishing from the banks are recommended to wear life jackets. Emergency buoys with ropes are location along the canal. This is a day-us area; no overnight camping is allowed.

Sutherland Reservoir

The Sutherland Reservoir is a 3,000-acre (12 km) lake located three miles (5 km) south of the Interstate 80 Exit at Sutherland, Neb. NPPD owns and manages the Sutherland Reservoir, part of its hydropower system. Nebraska Game and Parks Commission (NGPC) oversees most of the recreation areas at the lake. A day or season pass is required for entry into NGPC areas.

Primitive campsites are located on the east and west sides of the lake, while a private camping area with electrical hook-ups and a nine-hole golf course are located along the north shore. Four boat launching ramps and two swimming areas are available. NPPD maintains a roost and perch tree protection program for eagles and, during the winter months, bird watchers can observe numerous wintering American Bald Eagles.

North Platte Trail

In North Platte, the city's riding and hiking path continues on the south side of town along NPPD's North Platte Hydro tailrace canal. Trail users travel under Interstate 80 on a low-water bridge along the canal. Hikers and bikers pass along the grass and gravel canal maintenance road to State Farm Road where the route continues west. From the bridge, trail users receive a fine view of the North Platte Hydro. Fishing is allowed north of the bridge, but not immediately downstream of the North Platte Hydro. Boaters and swimmers are restricted from the tailrace canal.

Kearney Canal Trail

Kearney Dam and hydro plant

The City of Kearney and Buffalo County Parks and Recreation Department constructed an 8-foot (2.4 m)-wide concrete trail along NPPD's Kearney Canal in 1996. The 2.6-mile (4.2 km) scenic corridor is a gradual downhill grade from Cottonmill Park to the University of Nebraska at Kearney campus. The 16-mile (26 km)-long canal was built in the 1880s to divert Platte River water for irrigation and electrical generation. Cottonmill Lake once served as a reservoir for a cotton mill and now is a city park. The Kearney Dam & Hydro date to 1889. The 1.485-megawatt hydro-generator in the turret-looking tower was refurbished by NPPD in 1996. Access to NPPD's dam and hydro areas near the trail is restricted with no swimming or boating allowed.

Districts Served by NPPD

- Burt County PPD
- Butler PPD
- Cedar-Knox PPD
- Cuming County PPD
- Custer PPD
- Dawson PPD
- Elkhorn RPPD
- Howard-Greeley RPPD
- KBR RPPD
- Loup PPD
- Loup Valleys RPPD
- McCook PPD
- Niobrara Valley EMC
- Norris PPD
- North Central PPD
- Northeast NE PPD
- Perennial PPD
- Polk County PPD
- Seward County PPD
- South Central PPD
- Southern PD

- Southwest PPD
- Stanton County PPD
- Twin Valleys PPD

Wholesale Communities Served by NPPD

- Arapahoe
- Auburn
- Battle Creek
- Beatrice
- Bradshaw
- Brainard
- Central City
- Chester
- Cozad
- Davenport
- David City
- Deshler
- DeWitt
- Dorchester
- Edgar
- Fairmont
- Friend
- Giltner
- Gothenburg
- Hampton
- Hebron
- Hemingford
- Hildreth
- Holdrege
- Lexington
- Lodgepole
- Lyons
- Madison
- Minden
- Neligh
- Nelson
- North Platte
- Ord
- Polk
- Prague
- Randolph
- Scribner
- Seward
- Snyder
- South Sioux City
- Summerfield, KS
- Superior
- Sutton
- Valentine
- Wahoo
- Wakefield
- Walthill
- Wauneta
- Wayne
- Webber, KS
- Wilcox
- Wymore

Retail Communities Served by NPPD

- Ainsworth
- Alma
- Anoka
- Ashton
- Atkinson
- Aurora
- Barada
- Bassett
- Big Springs
- Bloomfield
- Brandon
- Bristow
- Broadwater
- Brule
- Burchard
- Butte
- Chadron
- Clinton
- Crab Orchard
- Craig
- Crawford
- Creighton
- Crystal Lake
- Dakota City
- Dawson
- DuBois
- Elm Creek
- Elsie
- Emmet
- Fort Robinson
- Geneva
- Gibbon
- Gordon
- Hartington
- Hay Springs
- Homer
- Humboldt
- Inman
- Kearney
- Lewellen
- Lewiston
- Lisco
- Long Pine
- Loup City
- Lynch
- Madrid
- McCook
- McGrew
- Meadow Grove
- Melbeta
- Merriman
- Milford
- Minatare
- Murray
- Mynard
- Nehawka
- Norfolk
- Northport
- Oakdale
- Oakland
- Odessa
- Ogallala
- Oglala Sioux
- O'Neill
- Oshkosh
- Pawnee City
- Pine Ridge
- Plattsmouth
- Ravenna
- Rushville
- St. Mary
- Scottsbluff
- Shelton
- Shubert
- Steinauer
- Stella
- Sterling
- Sutherland
- Table Rock
- Tekamah
- Terrytown
- Tilden
- Union
- Venango
- Verdon
- White Clay
- Whitney
- Winnebago
- York

Source (edited): "http://en.wikipedia.org/wiki/Nebraska_Public_Power_District"

Oglethorpe Power

Oglethorpe Power Corporation medium-sized electric utility in Georgia, United States. Formed in 1974,

Ogelthorpe is a not-for-profit cooperative owned by the 39 electric membership corporations that it serves. The utility's headquarters are in Tucker, Georgia. It is the largest power supply cooperative in the United States based upon assets and annual kilowatt-hour sales. The utility's service area covers 65 percent of the state of Georgia. However, Georgia Power is the largest electricity supplier in the state. Ogelthorpe co-own several of its plants with Georgia Power and the Municipal Electric Authority of Georgia. As of 2009, the utility has an annual revenue of $1.2 billion and assets of over $6 billion. In 1997, Ogelthorpe restructured into three separate, but interrelated, cooperatives. Oglethorpe Power Corporation handles electricity generation, Georgia Transmission Corporation owns and operates the transmission lines and substations and Georgia System Operations Corporation provides system and administrative support.

As of 2009, Oglethorpe's power plants had a combined capacity of 5,790 megawatts. About 23% of the capacity is coal, 46% natural gas, 19% nuclear and 12% hydroelectric power. It owns 633 megawatts of the 848-megawatt Rocky Mountain Hydroelectric Plant, a pure pumped-storage hydroelectric plant that stores energy during periods of low electricity demand and produces electricity during periods of high demand. The utility's nuclear power comes from its partial ownership of the Edwin I. Hatch Nuclear Generating Station and the Alvin W. Vogtle Electric Generating Plant. It has partial ownership of two coal plants and full ownership of a combined cycle power plant and several gas turbine power plants.
Source (edited): "http://en.wikipedia.org/wiki/Oglethorpe_Power"

Old Dominion Electric Cooperative

Old Dominion Electric Cooperative (ODEC) is an electric generation and transmission cooperative headquartered in Glen Allen, Virginia. ODEC provides wholesale power to its 11 member electric cooperatives in Virginia, Maryland, and Delaware. Through these member cooperatives, ODEC provided over 11 million megawatt hours of power to 1.4 million people in 2008. ODEC's member cooperatives primarily distribute power to rural, suburban, and recreation areas.

ODEC's generating facilities make use of coal, fuel oil, natural gas and nuclear energy. ODEC owns 11.6% of the North Anna Nuclear Generating Station in Louisa County. ODEC President Jack Reasor in 2007 stated that ODEC does not support a cap on carbon emissions as proposed by the United States Carbon Cap-and-Trade Program. In 2009, ODEC proposed building a coal plant in Dendron, Virginia.

Northern Virginia Electric Cooperative was a member of the cooperative until 31 December 2008, when it terminated its contract.

TEC Trading is a Class B member of Old Dominion and is owned by ODEC's member cooperatives. TEC purchases excess power from Old Dominion and sells it on the market.

Members
- A&N Electric Cooperative
- BARC Electric Cooperative
- Choptank Electric Cooperative
- Community Electric Cooperative
- Delaware Electric Cooperative
- Mecklenburg Electric Cooperative
- Northern Neck Electric Cooperative
- Prince George Electric Cooperative
- Rappahannock Electric Cooperative
- Shenandoah Valley Electric Cooperative
- Southside Electric Cooperative

Source (edited): "http://en.wikipedia.org/wiki/Old_Dominion_Electric_Cooperative"

Southern Maryland Electric Cooperative

The **Southern Maryland Electric Cooperative (SMECO)** is an electric distribution cooperative which is headquartered in Hughesville, Maryland. SMECO serves approximately 144,000 customers in Calvert, Charles, Prince George's, and St. Mary's counties of southern Maryland. Under its rules as a nonprofit cooperative, SMECO passes on its costs to its customer-members without markup or profit.

SMECO owns a 77 MW combustion turbine located at the Chalk Point Generating Station which, by an agreement until 2015, is operated and maintained by Mirant.

History

In 1937 two committees of citizens from three counties which were seeking aid to construct a local rural electric distribution system under the New Deal's Rural Electrictrification Administration formed the Southern Maryland Tri-County Electric Cooperative Association. This was reorganized as a cooperative under the SMECO name in 1942. Customers were allowed to select suppliers of electricity beginning in 2001 under the electric deregulation legislation enacted in 1999. SMECO has won the J.D. Power and Associates Award for best customer service for the East region midsize utility for the past three years.
Source (edited): "http://en.wikipedia.org/wiki/Southern_Maryland_Electric_Cooperative"

Utah Associated Municipal Power Systems

Utah Associated Municipal Power Systems is a governmental cooperative of municipalities, service districts, and political subdivisions that own their own public power systems. The Cooperative works to pool electrical energy resources to provide power to the various public power customers such as businesses and residents of the member utilities.

Nebo Power Station is owned by U.A.M.P.S.. It is a combined cycle natural gas fired 140 megawatt plant in Payson, Utah.

U.A.M.P.S. uses a variety of sources to meet the demand of its members with electrical supply. These include coal fired electrical plants, wind turbine electrical farms, hydroelectric power, and the Association's Nebo Power Station a natural gas combined cycle electrical plant.

The Association includes public entity members in Utah, Nevada, Idaho, Arizona, New Mexico, and California.

Source (edited): "http://en.wikipedia.org/wiki/Utah_Associated_Municipal_Power_Systems"

Wabash Valley Power Association

Wabash Valley Power Association is an electric generation and transmission cooperative headquartered in Indianapolis, Indiana. Wabash Valley provides wholesale power to 28 distribution cooperatives in Illinois, Indiana, Michigan and Missouri that reach over 350,000 businesses and residences. The cooperative operates under the business model of the National Rural Electric Cooperative Association.

Wabash Valley is a member of the PJM Interconnection and the Midwest Independent Transmission System Operator and a founding member of Touchstone Energy.

Wabash Valley's generating facilities make use of landfill gas generation, coal gasification and wind power. Their program for members to purchase energy from renewable sources is monickered EnviroWatts. In May 2009, Wabash Valley's Renewable Energy Certificate was certified by Green-e Energy.

Wabash Valley Power Association was founded in Peru, Indiana in 1963 by five distribution cooperatives. Their membership grew over the years and the headquarters were relocated to Indianapolis in 1976.

Members

- Boone REMC
- Carroll County REMC
- Central Indiana Power
- Citizens Electric Corporation
- Corn Belt Energy
- EnerStar Electric Cooperative
- Fulton County REMC
- Hendricks Power Cooperative
- Jasper County REMC
- Jay County REMC
- Kankakee Valley REMC
- Kosciusko REMC
- LaGrange County REMC
- M.J.M. Electric Cooperative
- Marshall County REMC
- Miami-Cass REMC
- Midwest Energy Cooperative
- Newton County REMC
- Noble REMC
- Northeastern REMC
- Parke County REMC
- Paulding-Putnam EC
- Steuben County REMC
- Tipmont REMC
- United REMC
- Wabash County REMC
- Warren County REMC
- White County REMC

Source (edited): "http://en.wikipedia.org/wiki/Wabash_Valley_Power_Association"

Alameda Municipal Power

Alameda Municipal Power (formerly Alameda Power & Telecom) is a municipal utility serving the City of Alameda, California. Founded in 1887, it provides electricity to approximately 34,000 residential, commercial, and municipal customers.

Known as being "The Greenest Little Utility in America," over 80% of Alameda Municipal Power's portfolio consists of renewable resources, including geothermal, hydroelectric, landfill gas, wind, and solar facilities.

Alameda residents pay no premium for this renewable power, and electric rates are typically lower than in surrounding communities. Alameda Municipal Power utility also provides a revenue stream to the City of Alameda, supporting municipal services and economic development efforts.

Source (edited): "http://en.wikipedia.org/wiki/Alameda_Municipal_Power"

American Public Power Association

The **American Public Power Association (APPA)** is the service organization for the more than 2,000 U.S. community-owned electric utilities that serve more than 45 million Americans.

APPA was created in September 1940 to represent the common interests of these utilities. Today, APPA's purpose is to advance the public policy interests of its members and their consumers and provide member services to ensure adequate, reliable electricity at a reasonable price with the proper protection of the environment.

Regular APPA membership is open to U.S. public power utilities, joint action agencies (state and regional consortia of public power utilities), rural electric cooperatives, Canadian municipal/provincial utilities, public power systems within U.S. territories and possessions, and state, regional, and local associations in the United States and Canada that have purposes similar to APPA. Members include Los Angeles Department of Water & Power, Long Island Power Authority, Salt River Project in Arizona, Sacramento Municipal Utility District, JEA in Florida, and Seattle City Light.

APPA also encourages associate memberships from entities and individuals that have an interest in doing business with public power, and from cities and towns exploring the possibility of establishing public power systems.

Activities

- APPA is the national advocate for public power in Washington, D.C., on legislative and regulatory issues, and in legal proceedings. APPA lobbies public power positions, and monitors and reports on federal events and activities. Its Legislative & Resolutions Committee gives all utility members an opportunity to develop consensus on issues, as do task forces, committees, and work groups. The annual Legislative Rally brings managers and policymakers to Washington, D.C., to tell the public power story.
- *Public Power Weekly* newsletter, *Public Power* magazine, and *Public Power Daily* are respected throughout the country as timely, reliable sources of information about public power and the industry. APPA's website provides information for a variety of audiences. Specialized publications, reports, surveys, and Internet-based networking groups inform and educate in various utility disciplines.
- APPA offers many opportunities to learn from and network with colleagues, utility experts, and local and national policymakers. The annual National Conference is the largest public power meeting. Other annual meetings cover business and financial, engineering and operations, legal, community broadband, and customer and community services topics. APPA also conducts smaller professional-development courses and provides a variety of continuing education and consumer-oriented materials.
- The Demonstration of Energy-Efficient Developments (DEED) program provides grants to APPA-member utilities and students from public power communities. Projects explore techniques and technologies that could be widely applicable to public power.
- Major awards are given at APPA's National Conference to executives and policymakers who have advanced public power's goals, as well as to utilities that have met the highest standards. Throughout the year, others are recognized for safety records, reliability, annual reports, lineworker skills, continuing education, and dedication to energy innovation.
- Hometown Connections, a subsidiary, secures group discounts for APPA members in a variety of areas, including advanced meter reading systems, customer information software, SCADA systems, broadband over powerline services, and customer and employee research.

Source (edited): "http://en.wikipedia.org/wiki/American_Public_Power_Association"

American Samoa Power Authority

The **American Samoa Power Authority (ASPA)** is a government-run public utility company headquartered in American Samoa.

The American Samoa Senate proposed the dissolution of the ASPA in 2008 due to financial difficulties. Under the bill, the ASPA would be dissolved and its assets and operations would be transferred to a new proposed American Samoa Utility Department. The Executive Branch would oversee the new American Samoa Utility Department if the proposal is adopted.

Source (edited): "http://en.wikipedia.org/wiki/American_Samoa_Power_Authority"

Austin Energy

Austin Energy is the public utility providing electrical power service to a 421-square-mile (1,090 km) area including Austin, Texas and parts of the surrounding area in Travis and Williamson counties. It has been owned by the City of Austin since its inception in 1893.

Power plants

- Holly Street Power Plant — Constructed 1960-1974, the Holly Street plant was designed to run on natural gas, with fuel oil as an alternative. At its peak, Holly produced up to 558 megawatts. Its location in a residential neighborhood resulted in considerable pressure to retire the plant, which occurred in 2007. The plant was decommissioned in September 2007 and will be deconstructed in the summer of 2010.
- Decker Creek Power Station — Constructed 1967-1978, the Decker Creek plant was designed to run on natural gas, with fuel oil as an alternative. The Decker Creek Power Station has an output of 926 megawatts.
- Sand Hill Energy Center — Constructed 2001-2004, the Sand Hill unit is a natural gas fired combined cycle power plant capable of generating 480 megawatts. Sand Hill Energy Center also has 4 natural gas simple cycle peaker units(LM6000) each capable of 50 megawatts. During the summer of 2009 work began on two new 50 megawatt simple cycle units. The project should be complete by the summer of 2010.
- Fayette Power Project — Austin Energy owns 50% of two units (Unit 1 and Unit 2) of this coal fired power plant, with the Lower Colorado River Authority
- South Texas Project — Austin Energy owns 16% of this nuclear power plant

Green energy

Energy customers can choose to pay a fixed 20 year rate on power obtained from renewable energy sources such as wind power by enrolling in the *GreenChoice* plan. Austin Energy purchases wind power generated in West Texas and power generated through the burning of landfill gas at landfills in Austin and San Antonio. As part of its *Power Saver* program, rebates of $2.50 per watt are offered for the purchase of solar photovoltaic cells. The utility has also offered rebates on some Energy Star appliances.

On March 5, 2009, the Austin City Council authorized Austin Energy to enter into an agreement with Gemini Solar Development Co. to build a 300-acre (1.2 km), 30 megawatt solar array. When completed in 2011, the plant, located in Webberville, Texas, will be the largest solar power generating project in the United States.

Source (edited): "http://en.wikipedia.org/wiki/Austin_Energy"

Brownsville Public Utilities Board

The **Brownsville Public Utilities Board**, or **Brownsville PUB**, is the main utility company in the city of Brownsville, Texas. It is the largest of three electric providers (in terms of local customers) in the city of Brownsville, as well as the largest water provider for the city.

Its electric division is currently the only city owned electric provider of any city in the Rio Grande Valley metropolitan area. It has operated since 1907 and currently owns three power plants and distributes power to approximately 1,300 miles of wires and 14 substations.

Source (edited): "http://en.wikipedia.org/wiki/Brownsville_Public_Utilities_Board"

Burlington Electric Department

The **Burlington Electric Department** (**BED**) is a municipally-owned electric utility located in Burlington, Vermont. It is the largest municipally-owned electric utility in Vermont. It has over 19,600 customers. It is the only utility providing electricity to the city and the Burlington International Airport, South Burlington.

Generating plants

It operates and owns 50% of a wood-powered electric generating facility. When this was constructed in 1984, it was the world's largest wood-burning generating plant. It still is one of the largest today.

The 30-megawatt coal-fired Moran Generating Station, named for Mayor J.E. Moran, was completed in 1954.

History

The utility was created in 1905, after city officials grew dissatisfied with the investor-owned Burlington Light and Power Company and its pricing.

Moran, a coal-fired plant was closed in the late 20th century. The city has planned to convert it to recreation or museum use.

Source (edited): "http://en.wikipedia.org/wiki/Burlington_Electric_Department"

CPS Energy

CPS Energy of San Antonio, Texas (formerly "City Public Service") is the United States' largest municipally owned utility company, with combined natural gas and electric service. Fourteen percent of all utility revenues are returned to the City of San Antonio, and those revenues make up more than 20 percent of the City of San Antonio's annual operating budget. Acquired by the City in 1942, CPS Energy serves over 707,000 electricity customers and more than 322,000 natural gas customers in its 1,566-square-mile (4,060 km) service area, which includes Bexar County and portions of 7 surrounding counties. CPS Energy's diverse fuel generation mix, including nuclear power (35%), coal (34%), natural gas (15%) and renewable energy (16 percent), makes energy affordable and reliable for its customers.

History
- 1917 - San Antonio Public Service Company formed; owned by American Light and Traction
- 1942 - City purchases SAPSCo for $34 million

Source (edited): "http://en.wikipedia.org/wiki/CPS_Energy"

Cedar Falls Utilities

The **Cedar Falls Utilities** (CFU) is a municipally-owned public utility company serving Cedar Falls, Iowa. CFU provides municipal water service, electricity generation and distribution, natural gas service, and combined cable television and Internet access to its customers.

CFU participates in municipal efforts to promote economic development, which in turn results in a larger customer base for its utility services. The utility donated land to form the Cedar Falls Industrial and Technology Park in the late 1960s and in more recent years has aggressively expanded access to its communications services, including cable television and broadband Internet access, which the city promotes as a key factor in its economic-development strategy. The communications utility began service in 1996 after a 1994 community referendum.

CFU was an early entrant into the market for renewable energy in the United States, investing in a wind-energy project in 1998 along with six other Iowa municipal utilities. CFU is projected to obtain 10% of its electricity from renewable sources by 2010.

Source (edited): "http://en.wikipedia.org/wiki/Cedar_Falls_Utilities"

City Utilities of Springfield

City Utilities of Springfield (CU) is a community-owned utility serving southwest Missouri with electricity, natural gas, water, telecommunications and transit services. CU provides service to over 106,000 customers.

CU is responsible for the generation, transmission, and distribution of electric power; the acquisition, transportation, and distribution of natural gas; and the acquisition, treatment, and distribution of water; plus the operation of the bus transportation system. The CU service territory covers approximately 320 square miles (830 km), which includes all of the city of Springfield, portions of Greene County, and a part of northern Christian County.

The utility is owned by the community and governed by an eleven-member Board of Public Utilities, nine of whom are customers inside the city limits and two who reside outside the city limits. Board members are appointed by City Council for three-year terms. The Board normally meets on the last Thursday of each month. The Board makes policy decisions for CU and appoints the General Manager, who is the Chief Executive Officer.

Source (edited): "http://en.wikipedia.org/wiki/City_Utilities_of_Springfield"

City Water, Light & Power

City Water, Light & Power is the largest municipally owned utility in the U.S. state of Illinois.

The utility provides the city of Springfield, Illinois with electric power from four coal-fired boilers. The boilers operate with water from the utility's wholly owned Lake Springfield, which also provides drinking water for the city.

The utility also owns much of the riparian property around Lake Springfield, some of which is preserved for local recreation and some of which is leased to local nonprofits, such as Lincoln Memorial Gardens.

The utility is currently attempting to construct a second reservoir, Hunter Lake.

Source (edited): "http://en.wikipedia.org/wiki/City_Water,_Light_%26_Power"

Cleveland Public Power

Cleveland Public Power (also known as **CPP**) is a publicly owned electricity generation and distribution company in

Ohio. It was founded in 1907 by Tom L. Johnson, then Mayor of Cleveland, Ohio. Before 1983 it was known as **Municipal Light** (or "**Muny Light**" for short). CPP does not have sufficient capacity to compete across the entire Greater Cleveland area. Rather, it is intended to create additional capacity and to create a benchmark price in order to prevent price gouging by local private utilities.

In December 1978, Mayor Dennis Kucinich refused to sell the company when a number of banks, which were heavily invested in Muny Light's privately owned competitor, the Cleveland Electric Illuminating Company (better known as CEI or The Illuminating Company) refused to roll over the city's debt, as had previously been customary. This was seen as a bad move at the time - unable to pay its debts, the city became the first since the Great Depression to enter default - but Kucinich's decision was later vindicated by both city officials and the U.S. Senate, which found that CEI and the banks had acted improperly.

In December 2006, a new commissioner for CPP, Ivan Henderson took over the reins from the incumbent James Majer. Under the new commissioner's guidance CPP is poised to take over the streetlight maintenance from CEI.

Source (edited): "http://en.wikipedia.org/wiki/Cleveland_Public_Power"

Eugene Water & Electric Board

The **Eugene Water & Electric Board (EWEB)** is the customer-owned electricity, water, and steam public utility provider for the city of Eugene, Oregon, United States. It is Oregon's largest customer-owned utility.

Source (edited): "http://en.wikipedia.org/wiki/Eugene_Water_%26_Electric_Board"

Florida Municipal Power Agency

The **Florida Municipal Power Agency (FMPA)** is a nonprofit, wholesale electric utilities and associated services company that serves its 30 Florida municipal electric utility system members. Based in Tallahassee, with its operational offices in Orlando FMPA is a governmental entity, established as a separate legal entity pursuant to interlocal agreement. FMPA's statutory authorization is found in section 163.01, Florida Statutes, and part II, chapter 361, Florida Statutes.

FMPA was created on February 24, 1978, by the signing of the Interlocal Agreement Creating the Florida Municipal Power Agency. Originally, 17 municipal electric utility systems were members of FMPA. FMPA was created largely in response to the Arab oil embargo that hit the U.S. economy hard in the 1970s. At that time, many of Florida's municipal electric utilities were trying to determine how to survive, and small cities needed the economies of scale that a larger organization could provide. With a $2 million seed money loan, the original members of FMPA created an organization to serve and support them, and to ensure the survival and vitality of Florida's municipal electric utilities in the future.

Member utilities
- Alachua
- Bartow
- Beaches Energy Services
- Blountstown
- Bushnell
- Clewiston
- Chattahoochee
- Fort Meade
- Fort Pierce Utilities Authority
- Gainesville Regional Utilities
- Green Cove Springs
- Havana
- Homestead Energy Services
- Key West
- Kissimmee Utility Authority
- Lake Worth
- Lakeland Electric
- Leesburg
- Moore Haven
- Mount Dora
- New Symrna Beach
- Newberry
- Ocala
- Orlando Utilities Commission
- Quincy
- Starke
- St. Cloud
- Vero Beach
- Wauchula
- Williston

Power Supply Projects

FMPA currently has five power supply projects:

All-Requirements Power Supply Project

The **All-Requirements Power Supply Project (ARP)** is FMPA's largest power supply project, and taken alone, is the fourth largest electric utility system in the state of Florida, with a peak demand of more than 1,600 MW. Fifteen of FMPA's member electric utility systems are currently participants in the ARP.

The ARP system stretches from Key West to the Town of Havana in the Florida Panhandle. While owning minimal transmission assets, FMPA is largely a transmission dependent utility, requiring access to, and use of, the electric transmission systems of large, vertically integrated investor-owned electric utilities.

The ARP system includes numerous generation facilities, including the ARP's newest generation facility—Treasure Coast Energy Center Unit 1 (TCEC1). TCEC1 is a nominal 300 MW combined cycle electric generation station. TCEC1 achieved commercial operation on May 30, 2008, and is the most efficient and cleanest power station in the State of Florida at this time. TCEC1's primary fuel is clean burning natural gas, but the unit also has the ability to burn fuel oil as a backup. TCEC1 was built from the ground-up by FMPA, a project that began in 2005. Fort Pierce Utilities Authority personnel operate TCEC1, working under a contractual arrangement with FMPA.

St. Lucie Project
The **St. Lucie Project** was the first FMPA power supply project. Fifteen of FMPA's members participate in the St. Lucie Project, which owns an 8.8% ownership interest in the Florida Power & Light St. Lucie Unit No. 2 nuclear plant, a nominally 838 MW generating facility.

Stanton Projects
- The **Stanton Project** owns a 14.8% share of the Stanton Unit No. 1, a 425 MW coal plant operated by OUC and located at the Curtis H. Stanton Energy Center in Orange County.
- • The **Tri-City Project** owns an additional 5.3% share of Stanton Unit No. 1. Three FMPA members participate in the Tri-City Project: Fort Pierce, Homestead, and Key West.
- The **Stanton II Project** owns a 23.2% share of Stanton Unit No. 2, a 429 MW coal plant operated by OUC and located at the Stanton Energy Center. Seven FMPA members participate in the Stanton II Project: Fort Pierce, Homestead, Key West, Kissimmee, St. Cloud, Starke, and Vero Beach.

Other projects
Initial Pooled Loan Project

Florida Joint Action Health Initiative

Governance
FMPA is governed by its Board of Directors. Each of FMPA's member systems is entitled to appoint one director and alternate directors to serve on the Board. The Board governs the business and affairs of FMPA generally, and each of FMPA's projects, except the All-Requirements Power Supply Project.

Each director (or his or her alternate acting in the place of the director) has at least one vote on all Board matters. Directors representing members that participate in a power supply project, but not the ARP get an additional one-half vote (thus, they may cast 1.5 votes). Directors representing members that participate in the ARP get one additional vote (thus, they may cast 2 votes).

ARP Governance
The ARP is governed by FMPA's Executive Committee. Each ARP Participant is entitled to appoint an Executive Committee member and alternates. The Executive Committee governs the business and affairs of the ARP and approves the FMPA general (non-projects) budget.

Management
There are four elected Board officers, two Executive Committee elected officers, and two appointed Board officers that, subject to the authority of the Board of Directors and the Executive Committee have charge over managing the business and affairs of FMPA. Elected officers of the Board and Executive Committee are elected each year at the annual meeting of FMPA's Board of Directors, which has always been held in conjunction with the FMEA-FMPA Annual Conference.

Currently, FMPA's elected Board Officers are:
Chairman - Vince Ruano (City of Bushnell)
Vice Chairman - Paul Kalv (City of Leesburg)
Secretary - Lou Hernandez (Key Energy Services)
Treasurer - Kevin McCarthy (City of Clewiston)
FMPA's elected Executive Committee officers are:
Chairperson - Thomas W. Richards (Fort Pierce Utilities Authority)
Vice Chairperson - Matthew Brower (City of Ocala)
FMPA's Board appointed officers are:
General Manager and CEO - Nicholas P. Guarriello
General Counsel and CLO - Frederick M. Bryant, Esquire
FMPA's senior management consists of:
Thomas E. Reedy - Assistant General Manager, Power Resources
Mark J. Larson - Assistant General Manager, Finance and CFO
Mark McCain - Assistant General Manager, Public Relations and Human Resources
Jody Lamar Finklea - Assistant General Counsel and Manager of Legal Affairs

Affiliated Organizations
Florida Municipal Electric Association, Inc. (FMEA)
The Energy Authority
Colectric Partners, Inc.
Public Gas Partners, Inc.
American Public Power Association
Source (edited): "http://en.wikipedia.org/wiki/Florida_Municipal_Power_Agency"

Holland Board of Public Works

The **Holland Board of Public Works** is a municipal utility in Holland, Michigan It provides electrical power drinking water and wastewater treatment. Its service area includes the city of Holland and parts of Park Township, Holland Charter Township, Fillmore Township and Laketown Township.

Electrical Generation
Electrical production began in 1893.

The current power plant, the James DeYoung, consists of three active units. Units 3, 4 and 5 range in capacity from 11 to 29.5 megawatts. They have a combined capacity of 60 megawatts. Units 1 and 2 are no longer in service. Coal delivered by boat is the plant's fuel source.

A 22 megawatt oil burning unit was built on Sixth Street in 1973.

In 1992, two peaking units were installed in the southside industrial park. Located on M-40 near the headquarters of office furniture manufacturer Haworth, each provides 34 megawatts of power and can burn natural gas or fuel oil. A 74 megawatt unit installed in 2000 burns natural gas only.

The BPW also owns shares in Consumers Energy's JH Campbell Unit 3 and Detroit Edison's Belle River Power Plant; power generated at these two plants is used to supplement power produced at the BPW's own facilities.

Water Filtration

Water from Lake Michigan is filtered at a facility in Park Township on the city's northside. The plant has a capacity of 38.5 million gallons per day. 230 miles (370 km) of pipe provide water to the City of Holland and portions of three neighboring townships (Park, Laketown and Holland Charter). There are four storage tanks and five pumping stations within the system.

Expansion has been considered by building a new plant south of the city near Saugatuck Dunes State Park.

Wastewater Treatment

Wastewater is treated at a facility on Lake Macatawa near the BPW's James DeYoung power plant. The plant spans both sides of River Avenue. Over 180 miles (290 km) of pipe and 36 lift stations are used on pipes up to 36 inches (910 mm) in diameter. Wastewater is collected from the City of Holland and portions of neighboring townships (Park, Laketown, Fillmore and Holland Charter).

Source (edited): "http://en.wikipedia.org/wiki/Holland_Board_of_Public_Works"

JEA

JEA (formerly Jacksonville Electric Authority), located in Jacksonville, Florida, is the eighth largest community-owned electric utility company in the United States and largest in Florida. As of 2009, JEA serves more than 417,000 electric customers, 305,000 water customers and 230,000 sewer customers. Besides Jacksonville (Duval County), JEA also has customers in Clay, Nassau and St. Johns counties.

History

The City of Jacksonville established an electric system in 1895. The electric system grew with the city, but remained a department of city government until an independent authority was created by the consolidation of city and county governments in 1967. During the 1970s, JEA's electric rates were among the highest in the nation. There were reports of customers with electric bills higher than their mortgage payments.

Royce Lyles became JEA Managing Director on September 1, 1979 and the utility began diversifying its fuel mix. Rates began to *drop*, eventually becoming the lowest in the state and near the bottom in the Southeast. JEA became an admired and respected organization. Walt Bussells was appointed Managing Director on September 8, 1995, following Royce Lyles' retirement.

Jacksonville's water and sewer systems had been operated by the city since 1880. On June 1, 1997, the City of Jacksonville, Department of Public Utilities, water and sewer operations merged into JEA. Since the Jacksonville Electric Authority was also operating other utilities, they requested a name change to the initials, *JEA*; the City Council approved it on September 23, 1998, effectively making JEA an orphan acronym. Walt Bussells embraced new technology and in 2002, JEA introduced online bill payment and implemented network meter reading. In 2003, the utility also began providing Chilled water for air conditioning in downtown buildings. The first two customers were the downtown library and the John Milton Bryan Simpson United States Courthouse. Purchasing chilled water eliminates the need for chillers and cooling towers at each property, reducing capital outlays and eliminating ongoing maintenance costs. The space saved can also become rentable, increasing revenue.

Jim Dickenson replaced Walt Bussells when Bussells retired in 2004.

Services

- Electricity: owns/operates three generating plants and all transmission and distribution facilities; co-owns two additional power plants with Florida Power & Light: the St. Johns River Power Park in northeastern Jacksonville; and Unit 4 of Plant Scherer, near Macon, Georgia. JEA also operates a methane-fueled generating facility at the Girvin Road Landfill.
- Water: 134 artesian wells tapping the Floridan Aquifer are distributed through 35 water treatment plants and 4,208 miles (6,772 km) of water lines.
- Sewer: 3,760 miles (6,050 km) of collection lines and seven regional and eight non-regional sewage treatment plants.
- Chilled water: the company owns one chiller plant in downtown Jacksonville which provides the commodity to nearby facilities to heat and cool their buildings' air and equipment.

Current issues

Since 2004, JEA has assessed fuel rate increases three times. In 2007, JEA had the second-lowest electric rates in Florida before they announced a four-year base rate increase package that will bring the average bill from $112 to more than $140 in 2010. Most utilities had been forced to raise their rates due to increased fuel costs, but approved rate increases were designed to reduce the utility's debt, currently at $6.0 billion compared to assets of $7.5 billion. Compared to other similar sized municipal utilities, JEA has 60% more debt per customer, which can lower the util-

Kissimmee Utility Authority

Kissimmee Utility Authority was founded in 1901 and is Florida's sixth largest municipally-owned utility providing electric and telecommunication services to 64,000 customers in Osceola County, Florida. KUA owns and operates the Roy E. Hansel Generating Station and the Cane Island Power Park and has ownership interests in other generating stations, including coal, natural gas and nuclear sources.

KUA holds responsibility for customer service, meter reading and billing services for Toho Water Authority, under a management contract. KUA also provides billing for refuse and storm water services for the City of Kissimmee, Florida.

Hurricanes Charley, Frances and Jeanne

In 2004, KUA and its employees experienced seven of the most devastating weeks in the utility's 103-year history when three major hurricanes struck its service area. KUA was the hardest hit electric utility in Central Florida, having lost electric service to 100 percent of its customers in Hurricane Charley, 36 percent in Hurricane Frances and 59 percent in Hurricane Jeanne. KUA workers logged 16-hour days trimming trees, digging holes, setting poles, pulling wires and restoring electricity to tens of thousands of Osceola County residents.

Criticized by customers and some local government officials about communication on power restoration efforts after Hurricane Charley, KUA's board of directors called for an independent evaluation by consulting firm James Lee Witt Associates of Washington, D.C., in December. The report by the company headed by the director of the Federal Emergency Management Administration for eight years stated that KUA should improve its emergency preparedness plan and communication.

Board of directors

As of October 2010
- Fred H. Cumbie, Jr., chairman
- James R. Kasper, vice chairman
- Reginald L. Hardee, secretary
- Dr. George A. Gant, assistant secretary
- Kathleen Thacker, director
- Jim Swan (Mayor of Kissimmee, ex-officio member)

Executive Management

- James C. Welsh, President & General Manager
- Kenneth L. Davis, Vice President of Engineering & Operations
- Chris M. Gent, Vice President of Corporate Communications
- Jeffery S. Gray, Vice President of Information Technology
- Wilbur D. Hill, Vice President of Human Resources
- Joseph Hostetler, Vice President of Finance & Risk Management
- Arthur J. "Grant" Lacerte, Jr., Vice President and General Counsel
- Larry W. Mattern, Vice President of Power Supply
- Susan C. Postans, Vice President of Customer Service
- Gregory D. Woessner, Vice President of System Compliance and Operations

Source (edited): "http://en.wikipedia.org/wiki/Kissimmee_Utility_Authority"

Lansing Board of Water & Light

The **Lansing Board of Water and Light** is a publicly owned, municipal utility that provides electricity and water to the residents of the cities of Lansing and East Lansing, Michigan and the surrounding townships of Delta, Delhi, Meridian and DeWitt. The Lansing Board of Water and Light also provides steam and chilled water services within the City of Lansing.

History

The Lansing Board of Water and Light is a municipal utility, owned by the citizens of Lansing, Michigan. The utility's roots go back to 1885, when Lansing citizens approved a $100,000 bond issue to build a water system to provide for drinking water and fire protection. Electricity was added to its list of utility services in 1892, and steam heat in 1919.

System Information

The Lansing Board of Water and light has an electric generating capacity of 510 megawatts. The LBWL's transmission line voltage is 138,000 volts. The LBWL's distribution voltages are 13,200 volts, 8,320 volts and 4,160 volts.

The Lansing Board of Water and Light pumps an average of approximately 23 Million Gallons per Day (MGD) from two conditioning plants through approximately 775 miles (1,247 km) of water main. Maximum daily demand is on the order of 33 MGD, while the maximum hourly demand rate can be on the order of 42 MGD. Raw water is obtained exclusively by pumping from 124 wells located throughout the Lansing area. All system pressure is generated via pumping; the Lansing Board of Water and Light does not maintain any elevated water storage tanks.

Water Utility

The Lansing Board of Water and Light obtains all raw water from a series of

124 wells located throughout the city of Lansing, making it one of the few public utilities for large cities that provides water exclusively from wells. The city sits atop, and draws its water from, the Saginaw Aquifer, a natural underground reservoir 4 cubic miles, and 550 square miles in size. The raw water is pumped directly to two conditioning plants; the John Dye plant located in downtown Lansing, and the Wise Road plant located on the southwest side of the city. At these plants, water hardness is reduced by adding lime and soda ash to the water, which reacts with dissolved calcium and magnesium to form calcium carbonate and magnesium hydroxide floc. The floc then settles out of the water in large settling basins, and any residual floc is removed via sand and gravel filtering. This process reduces the hardness of the water from approximately 411 parts per million (ppm) to about 85 ppm. The finished water is then chlorinated and fluorinated, and sent to storage prior to distribution.

At the John Dye conditioning plant, two pumping stations located on the north and south sides of the plant draw finished water from three ground level storage facilities and pump to the distribution system. The Dye pump station, located on the south side of the conditioning plant, pumps water to the north towards Dewitt Township, Bath Township, and Watertown Township, to the west to Delta Township, and to the local distribution system. The Cedar Street pump station provides supplemental pumping capacity during periods of high demand. The Wise Road conditioning plants similarly pumps water directly into the distribution system, and generally feeds portions of Windsor Township, Delhi Township, and Alaiedon Township. Using a series of normally closed valves and booster stations, a pressure boundary exists roughly along I-96.

The Lansing Board of Water and Light retail customers consist of residential, commercial and industrial customers within the service areas, totalling approximately 56,000 customers. Approximately 48,000 of these customers are residential, 7,000 commercial, while the remaining customers consist of industrial customers. In addition, the Lansing Board of Water and Light sells water on a wholesale basis the local distribution systems in Delta Township and Meridian Township.

Electric Utility

Otto E. Eckert Station.

LBWL's largest power plant is the **Otto E. Eckert Station**, and was named after the utility's general manager from 1927 to 1966. The coal-fired generating station is located in downtown Lansing on the Grand River adjacent to General Motors' Grand River Assembly Plant, and the now-demolished Lansing Car Assembly Plant. Begun in 1922 and completed the following year, the power station has undergone numerous expansions and additions since, with the addition of the three chimneys in 1981. The station has a generating capacity of 351MW, produced by burning coal from Wyoming's Powder River Basin. This plant has three 615-foot (187 m) smokestacks, the tallest self supporting structures in south central Michigan. These stacks are visible from fifteen miles (24 km) on a clear day. The stacks are known locally by the names of Wynken, Blynken, and Nod, after the fishermen in a poem of the same name by Eugene Field. It was announced in May 2008 that the plant is scheduled for a phased decommissioning that is scheduled to begin in 2017 and end in 2025.

The LBWL's secondary generating plant is the **Claud R. Erickson Station**, named after general manager of the utility from 1966 to 1972. The plant located in Delta Township on Canal Road just south of Mt. Hope. This plant, built in 1973, is coal-fired and has a single generating unit with a capacity of 159 megawatts and is connected to the power grid by three 138,000 volt lines.

The utility's power plant inventory once included the 25 megawatt **Ottawa Street Station** on the Grand River in downtown Lansing. This steam and electrical plant operated from its completion in 1940 until 1992, when it was decommissioned as a power station, with steam and electrical production transferred to the Eckert Station. The station was put back into partial usage as a water chiller plant for the utility in 2001 to cool downtown buildings. In late 2007, LBWL sold the most vacant station to Accident Fund Insurance Company, national insurance company, to be renovated into their headquarters. At the end of December of that year, in preparation for the renovation, the iconic smokestack portion of the building was taken down.

During periods of high demand, the Lansing Board of Water and light purchases 146 megawatts of electricity from Detroit Edison's Belle River Power Plant located in East China Township, Michigan, south of Port Huron. The LBWL has two 138KV interconnections (Davis-Oneida line and the Davis-Enterprise line) with Consumers Energy/METC from its substation on Jolly Road just east of Pennsylvania Ave on Lansing's south side.

Source (edited): "http://en.wikipedia.org/wiki/Lansing_Board_of_Water_%26_Light"

Long Island Power Authority

The **Long Island Power Authority** or LIPA ["lie-pah"], a municipal subdivision of the State of New York, was created under the Long Island Power Act of 1985 to acquire the Long Island Lighting Company (LILCO)'s assets and securities. A second Long Island Power Authority (LIPA), a wholly owned subsidiary of the first, acquired LILCO's transmission and distribution system in May 1998.

LIPA, a non-profit municipal electric utility, owns the retail electric system on Long Island and provides electric service to over 1.1 million customers in Nassau and Suffolk counties, and the Rockaway Peninsula in Queens. LIPA does not own any electric generation assets on Long Island, and it does not provide natural gas service.

National Grid USA, previously Keyspan Energy, maintains LIPAs transmission and distribution system under a management services agreement.

LIPA's transmission voltages are 345,000, 138,000 and 69,000 volts, sub-transmission voltages are 33,000 and 23,000 volts, and distribution voltages are 13,200 and 4,000 volts.

On January 24, 2007, then-Governor Eliot Spitzer announced that Kevin Law would replace Richard Kessel as Chairman of LIPA until the fall when a new Chairman would be named and Law would become Chief Executive Officer of LIPA. On October 8, 2007, Law took over as President and CEO.

Kevin Law stepped down on September 1, 2010 in order to become the new President of the Long Island Association. Chief Operating Officer Michael Hervey assumed the responsibilities until a new CEO and President is selected by the LIPA Board of Trustees.

Source (edited): "http://en.wikipedia.org/wiki/Long_Island_Power_Authority"

Los Angeles Department of Water and Power

The **Los Angeles Department of Water and Power** (LADWP) is the largest municipal utility in the United States, serving over four million residents. It was founded in 1902 to supply water and electricity to residents and businesses in Los Angeles and surrounding communities. The LADWP receives no tax support, and contributes about $190 million annually to the revenues of the city of Los Angeles.

History

Private operators

By the middle of the 19 century, Los Angeles's rapid population growth magnified problems with the city's water distribution system. At that time a system of open ditches, often polluted, was reasonably effective at supplying water to agriculture but was not suited to providing water to homes. In 1853, the city council rejected as "excessive" a closed-pipe system that would serve homes directly. As a solution, the city allowed "water carriers with jugs and horse-drawn wagons…to serve the city's domestic [water] needs". It took until 1857 for the council to realize that the system needed to be updated, which led them to grant William G. Dryden franchise rights to provide homes with water through a system of underground water mains. The initial system served only a few homes using an unreliable network of wooden pipes. In December 1861, heavy rains destroyed the system and Dryden gave up his franchise. The city attempted contracting out water distribution rights to others, but none of the systems that resulted from these contracts was successful.

The city's previous unsuccessful attempts to allow others to develop a water system on its behalf prompted the city council to relinquish its rights to the water in the Los Angeles River in 1868, benefited John S. Griffen, Solomon Lazard, and Prudent Beaudry, three already successful businessmen. This change was at the expense of the city of Los Angeles, which could no longer benefit from their municipal water distribution business. The three men created the Los Angeles City Water Company, which violated many of the provisions of its lease on the Los Angeles River, including secretly tunneling under the river to extract 150 times as much water as the lease allowed. As a result, as the end of the lease drew near in the mid-1890s, "popular support began to build for a return to complete municipal control of the local water supply".

Public control

The John Ferraro Building, LADWP Headquarters in Downtown Los Angeles

The leader in the fight to end private control of the water supply was Fred Eaton. Eaton proposed that tax revenues would enable the city of Los Angeles to provide water to its residents without charging them for the use of water directly. Eaton's views were especially powerful because of "his distinguished record of achievement rendered in both the private and public sector". During Eaton's nine-year term as the superintending engineer of the Los Angeles City Water Company, he headed a large expansion of the company's water system. Eaton left his position in 1886 when he was elected City Engineer. In his new public position, Eaton devoted his time to the updating and expansion of the sewer system. Eaton felt that the Los Angeles City Water Company was not serving the citizens of Los Angeles in the best way possible because of high rates and the fact the company frequently paid dividends to its stockholders instead of improving the water system. In early 1897, city engineers began creating plans for an updated water system while the city council informed the Los Angeles City Water Company that its lease would not be renewed beyond its expiration date, July 21, 1898. In early 1898, the city began talks with the Los Angeles City Water Company about taking over the company's current water system.

Throughout the negotiations, it became clear that it was necessary for the current senior employees of the Los Angeles City Water Company to keep their jobs in order to ensure that the water system could continue to operate. It was not guaranteed, however, that William Mulholland, Eaton's protégé and the man who took over the job of superintending engineer when Eaton was elected city engineer, would have a position working with the city-owned water system. Mulholland was not popular with city officials because he did not produce records that the city requested during negotiations. Near the end of the talks between the city and the water company, it was discovered that neither the requested records nor a map of the water system existed. Mulholland, who was supposed to be in charge of the non-existent records, was never a fan of paperwork and claimed that he had memorized all of the necessary information, including "the size of every inch of pipe and the age and location of every valve". Mulholland secured a job with the city when he successfully demonstrated his ability to recall the information. Once Mulholland was assured a job with the city, he "promptly intervened with the company's principal stockholder, advising him to accept the city's offer of two million dollars for the system".

Power delivery
The LADWP first offered municipal electricity in 1917 when the San Francisquito Power Plant began generating electricity. It ultimately produced 70.5 megawatts and is still in operation in 2004, producing 44.5 megawatts.

On January 17, 1994, the city of Los Angeles experienced its one and only total system black-out as a result of the Northridge Earthquake. Much of the power was restored within a few hours.

The California power crisis of 2001 had very little impact on the citizens of Los Angeles due to the LADWP's conservative approach to electricity deregulation.

Notable events and controversies
In 1928, the St. Francis Dam, built and operated by the LADWP, collapsed catastrophically. Over four hundred-fifty people died in the immediate vicinity, but the overall death toll was mitigated by prompt warnings sent to downriver communities in the Santa Clara River Valley, including Fillmore, Santa Paula, and San Buenaventura. Mulholland assumed full responsibility for the disaster and retired. The pall of the disaster hung over him until his death in 1935.

The LADWP has been a leading actor in the struggle over access to water from the Owens Valley, starting with its initial acquisition of water rights, as well as buying out farms and asserting control over Mono Lake and Owens Lake.

The LADWP and William Mulholland played a key role in the development of Hoover Dam and bringing its energy to Los Angeles. The LADWP continued to operate the Hoover Dam electrical facility until 1987.

Service territory
In addition to the city of Los Angeles, LADWP also provides services to these communities:
- Bishop (parts of)
- Culver City (parts of)
- South Pasadena (parts of)
- West Hollywood (parts of)

Operational systems

Power system
The LADWP currently maintains a generating capacity of 7,200 megawatts, in excess of the peak demand of 6,165 megawatts by the city of Los Angeles. It provides this surplus electricity to other utilities, selling 23 million megawatt-hours in 2003. As of 2005, the LADWP operates four natural gas-fired generators within city boundaries, which account for 26% of capacity. It receives 52% of its electricity from coal-fired plants in Utah, Arizona, and Nevada. A further 11% is generated using nuclear power. It receives about 6% of its electricity from hydropower, most coming from Hoover Dam and the rest coming from the aqueduct system itself as the water descends from its mountain sources.

The LADWP, along with the California Department of Water Resources, also operates the Castaic Pumped Storage Power Station as a pumped storage facility. Water flows from the upper reservoir to the lower during the day, generating power when demand is highest, and is pumped back up at night when excess capacity is available. About 1,600 megawatts, or 22% of the total capacity, is generated at this facility alone . The Los Angeles City Council voted in 2004 to direct the LADWP to generate 20% of its energy (excluding Hoover Dam) from clean sources by 2010 . Current "green power" sources account for 5% of the LADWP's capacity, but there are plans to add a 120 megawatt wind farm in Tehachapi, California, and produce electricity from geothermal sources in the Salton Sea area and photovoltaic sources.

Because Los Angeles is older than most other cities in California, the LADWP is currently faced with several unique issues. Most of the power lines in Los Angeles were built above-ground before it became customary to run power lines below-ground; as a result, the horizon line of the typical Los Angeles boulevard looks much more cluttered than boulevards in most Southern California cities. LADWP has been continuing a long-term project to convert overhead power lines to underground. This difficult conversion has been slowed by budget constraints, the impact on traffic, the pursuit of other modernization projects, and the lingering effects of a workforce reduction over the last decade. Budget issues are particularly acute in the department's transmission system, where underground transmission costs about 10 to 14 times the cost of overhead transmission, per unit length, and the technical and environmental challenges which confront such installations. The department recently completed two 230 kV underground projects using an innovative cable technology which does not utilize oil as an insulator. The oilless cable mitigates the environmental issues associated with oil-type cable.

Water system

The LADWP provided more than 200 billion US gallons (760 billion liters) of water in 2003, pumping it through 7,226 miles (11,629 km) of pipe. In fiscal year 2004-2005:
- 48% of the water came from the Sierra Nevada mountains via the Los Angeles Aqueduct;
- 41% came from the Metropolitan Water District of Southern California, which transports water from the California Aqueduct and Colorado River Aqueduct;
- 11% was from local groundwater, a resource that is actively managed and allocated, but is continually being threatened by chemical pollutants, such as MTBE and perchlorates;
- 1% came from recycled water and was used for irrigation, recreation, and industrial purposes.

The use of water from specific sources can vary greatly from year to year.

The prospect of increased demand coupled with reduced supply from the Mono and Owens basins is causing the LADWP look into a number of new water sources, including a new direct connection to the California Aqueduct, increased use of recycled water, use of stormwater capture and reuse, and increased conservation. Many of the old pipelines are beginning to wear out, or are at capacity and insufficient to handle future demand. LADWP has undertaken pipeline replacement projects on many L.A. boulevards like Exposition and Olympic, but the necessary lane closures have only worsened the city's chronic traffic congestion.

Media portrayals

Unusual for a municipal public utility, LADWP has been mentioned several times in popular culture, both fiction and nonfiction:
- The 1974 Roman Polanski film *Chinatown* sets its story around LADWP's efforts to acquire land and water rights.
- In 1982 the University of California Press published William L. Kahrl's book *Water and Power: The Conflict over Los Angeles' Water Supply in the Owens Valley* (ISBN 0-520-04431-2). The book examined the development of water policy in the American West, particularly concentrating on the role of William Mulholland and the LADWP.
- The 1986 book *Cadillac Desert: The American West and its Disappearing Water* by Marc Reisner (ISBN 0-14-017824-4) is about land development and water policy in the western United States. The subsequent television documentary of the same name devotes an entire episode to *Mulholland's Dream* to provide plentiful water for Los Angeles.
- The 1995 movie *Mighty Morphin Power Rangers: The Movie* makes reference to the Los Angeles Department of Water and Power. The movie takes place in a fictional city modeled after Los Angeles. In one of the movie's scenes, after finding a mysterious object in the ground on a construction site, one construction worker asks another, "what in the world is this?" The other construction worker replies "well it sure as heck ain't DWP."
- In the 2009 ABC television series *FlashForward*, the exterior of the LADWP headquarters is used to portray the FBI field office building where several main characters are based.
- In the 2009 movie *Obsessed* the building was also featured.
- The 2010 Christopher Nolan film *Inception* features the LADWP headquarters, though a noticeably taller version. The building was shown in the world created by the protagonist and antagonist during a decades-long shared dream.

Source (edited): "http://en.wikipedia.org/wiki/Los_Angeles_Department_of_Water_and_Power"

Memphis Light, Gas and Water

The **Memphis Light, Gas and Water Division** (MLGW) is the largest three-service municipal utility in the U.S. with more than 420,000 customers. Since 1939, MLGW has provided electricity, natural gas and water service for Memphis, Tennessee and Shelby County residents.

MLGW is supplied with electricity by the Tennessee Valley Authority (TVA), a federal agency that sells electricity on a nonprofit basis to its distributors. MLGW is TVA's largest customer, representing 11 percent of TVA's total load. There are over 428,000 electric customers.

Natural gas is the most common means of residential heating in the MLGW service area. MLGW provides natural gas to more than 313,000 customers in Shelby County.

While some utilities obtain drinking water from surface lakes or rivers, MLGW supplies water from the Memphis aquifer beneath Shelby County. It contains more than 100 trillion gallons of water that are more 2000 years old. MLGW operates one of the largest artesian well systems in the world consisting of 10 water pumping stations and more than 175 wells, delivering water to more than 253,000 customers.

Source (edited): "http://en.wikipedia.org/wiki/Memphis_Light,_Gas_and_Water"

Nashville Electric Service

Nashville Electric Service is among the twelve largest public electric utilities in the nation, currently employing a little over 1000 employees, and distributing energy to more than 350,000 customers in Middle Tennessee. The NES service area covers 700 square miles (1,800 km), all of Davidson County and portions of the six surrounding counties.

The 5 member Electric Power Board of the Metropolitan Government of Nashville and Davidson County (the "Power Board") was established in 1939 when TVA purchased TEPCO or Tennessee Electric Power Co. for 79 million dollars. After the purchase, the five hundred employees of TEPCO become employees of the newly created Nashville Electric Service.

NES is the operating name of the Electric Power Board of the Metropolitan Government of Nashville and Davidson County. The five member Board is appointed by the Mayor and confirmed by the Council. Members of the Board serve five-year staggered terms without pay. The Board appoints a chief executive officer who has responsibility for day-to-day operations, including hiring of employees.

Source (edited): "http://en.wikipedia.org/wiki/Nashville_Electric_Service"

New York Power Authority

The **New York Power Authority** (NYPA), officially the Power Authority of the State of New York (PASNY), is a New York State public benefit corporation and the largest state-owned power organization in the United States. NYPA provides some of the lowest-cost electricity in New York State, operating 17 generating facilities and more than 1,400 circuit-miles of transmission lines. It is based in White Plains.

The New York Power Authority sells electric power to government agencies, community-owned electric systems and rural electric cooperatives, companies, private utilities for resale (without profit) to their customers, and to neighboring states, under federal requirements.

Governor Franklin D. Roosevelt established New York's model for public power through legislation signed in 1931. This effort to secure public control of New York's hydropower resources was the result of a bipartisan effort that began with Governor Charles Evans Hughes in 1907.

NYPA operates hydro-electric complexes at the Niagara Power Project on the Niagara River, the St. Lawrence-FDR Project on the St. Lawrence River and the Blenhein-Gilboa pumped-storage hydro plant in the Catskill Mountains, producing a total of 4.2 million kilowatts of electricity. Each has a visitor center open to the public.

In November 2000, Entergy Corporation purchased the Fitzpatrick and Indian Point Unit 3 nuclear power plants from NYPA.

Source (edited): "http://en.wikipedia.org/wiki/New_York_Power_Authority"

Orlando Utilities Commission

The **Orlando Utilities Commission** (**OUC**: "The *Reliable* One") is a municipally-owned public utility providing water and electric service to the citizens of Orlando, Florida and portions of adjacent unincorporated areas of Orange County, as well as St. Cloud, Florida, in Osceola County. OUC currently serves more than 250,000 customers.

Chartered in 1923, OUC is the second largest locally owned electric utility in Florida and the 16th largest in the nation. The company is governed by a five-member commission (including the Mayor of Orlando), which is responsible for all operating policies.

OUC owns and operates the Curtis H. Stanton Energy Center and portions of other power plants in Florida. Notable ownership includes the Indian River Plant north of Cocoa, a former OUC plant now owned by RRI Energy; as well as a 6.08% stake in the St. Lucie Nuclear Power Plant near Fort Pierce.

OUC also owns eight water plants.

Source (edited): "http://en.wikipedia.org/wiki/Orlando_Utilities_Commission"

Sacramento Municipal Utility District

The **Sacramento Municipal Utility District** (**SMUD**) provides electricity to Sacramento County, California, and a small portion of adjacent Placer County, established under the Municipal Utility District Act. It is one of the ten largest publicly owned utilities in the United States, generating the bulk of its power through natural gas (estimated 56% of production total in 2009) and large hydroelectric generation plants (22% in 2009), and SMUD's green power (renewable) energy output was estimated as 19% in 2009.

SMUD's headquarters building, built

in the late 1950s on the edge of the East Sacramento neighborhood, is notable for its mural by Sacramento artist Wayne Thiebaud. The mural wraps around the ground floor of the building and is accessible to the public. It is one of the earliest major works by the artist, and remains his largest installation to date.

History

Created by a vote of Sacramento County residents in 1923, SMUD's ability to provide power to its customer-owners was stymied in the courts for nearly a quarter century by the investor-owned Pacific Gas & Electric Company (PG&E) of San Francisco. A court ruling eventually sided with SMUD, which began providing power at the beginning of 1946. SMUD is a public agency of the State of California, and as such is not subject to the Federal Energy Regulatory Commission's jurisdiction under the Federal Power Act. Echoes of SMUD's fight to fulfill its original mandate from the voters have continued in more recent turf battles with PG&E. In the 1980s, residents of Folsom voted to join SMUD, with PG&E fighting the annexation in the courts. Folsom rate-payers are now part of SMUD. In 2006, PG&E successfully convinced SMUD rate-payers and rate-payers in Yolo County to vote down an annexation proposal that would have extended the public utility's service territory to include the Yolo County cities of West Sacramento, Davis and Woodland, along with territory between the three cities.

SMUD's electricity generation capacity consists in part of hydroelectric plants on the American River. The plants are run during hours of peak demand, though retaining sufficient flood control capacity dictates water releases to some extent. SMUD also owns the first of potentially two natural gas power plants (the Cosumnes Power Plant, brought online in 2006 on property adjacent to the decommissioned Rancho Seco nuclear facility) as well as wind-powered and solar-powered electric generation facilities. In addition, the utility owns some small gas-fired peaker plants for meeting the highest energy demands, typically on Sacramento's notably blistering summer days.

SMUD owned the Rancho Seco nuclear power plant, shut down by a vote of the utility's rate-payers in the late 1980s. Although the nuclear plant is now decommissioned, its now-empty iconic towers remain on the site. Solar arrays and the 500 megawatt Cosumnes gas-fired plant have risen in proximity to the towers.

PHEV Research Center

SMUD is in the Advisory Council of the PHEV Research Center.

Source (edited): "http://en.wikipedia.org/wiki/Sacramento_Municipal_Utility_District"

Salt River Project

The **Salt River Project (SRP)** is the umbrella name for two separate entities: the **Salt River Project Agricultural Improvement and Power District**, an agency of the state of Arizona that serves as an electrical utility for the Phoenix metropolitan area, and the **Salt River Valley Water Users' Association**, a utility cooperative that serves as the primary water provider for much of central Arizona. It is one of the primary public utility companies in Arizona.

The name, *Rio Salado Project*, (Spanish for Salt River Project) is used to refer to the improvement projects along the Salt River through the Phoenix Metropolitan Area, is not related to SRP.

Service territory

SRP serves nearly all of the Phoenix metropolitan area. A large chunk of its electric service territory is shared with Arizona Public Service.

Governance

The Association is headed by a 10-member board and a 30-member council, while the District is headed by a 14-member board and a 30-member council. Both are elected by all landowners in the SRP service area through a "debt-proportionate" system. For instance, a person who owns five acres casts five votes.

History

Early settlers in Phoenix and nearby areas were forced to depend upon the flow of the Salt River to sustain agricultural activities. The river was prone to both floods and droughts and proved to be a less than reliable resource for the settlers. Failed plans to build a dam on the river in 1897, combined with a series of droughts, heightened the need for controlling the river.

With the passage of the National Reclamation Act of 1902, funding for reclamation projects with low-interest government loans paved the way for the creation of the Salt River Valley Water Users' Association the following year. Over 200,000 acres (800 km²) of private land belonging to the ranchers and farmers in the association were pledged for collateral and the association was officially incorporated February 7, 1903, becoming the first multipurpose project under the reclamation act. Construction on the Roosevelt Dam would commence the following year.

The original **Roosevelt Dam**, completed in 1911, was the highest masonry dam ever built. In 1996, it was upgraded by encasing the original construction in new concrete (shown).

Although the construction of dams

was the association's most visible and costly project, an integral part of the effort was also the construction and improvement of a system of canals designed to distribute the water from the Salt River among the various members living in the valley.

In 1909, a hydroelectric generator was installed at Roosevelt Dam; and, since that day, SRP has also been a major player in the power generation business.

In 1936, the Arizona Legislature allowed for the creation of governmental districts that could finance large-scale agricultural projects with tax-free bonds. Shortly thereafter, the Salt River Project Agricultural Improvement and Power District was created, the second half of SRP as it exists today. Over the next several decades, a series of major improvements along the Salt and Verde rivers would raise the number of reservoirs in the district to six, and at the same time SRP was constructing and maintaining a number of other electrical generating stations throughout the state.

As of 2007, SRP owns or operates eleven electrical generating stations, seven hydroelectric plants, and has energy purchasing agreements with four major hydroelectric stations along the Colorado River, making them a major provider of electric service in the Phoenix area. Along with the six reservoirs along the Salt and Verde rivers, SRP operates dams at the Blue Ridge Reservoir as well as the Granite Reef Diversion Dam and a number of canals, making the SRP a major provider of water to the Phoenix area.

Salt River reservoirs

SRP owns and operates four reservoirs along the Salt River east of Phoenix. While the main function of these reservoirs is to serve as water storage for the rapidly growing municipal area, they also serve as important recreational centers. The lakes are regularly stocked with fish, and are supplied with boat ramps for both angling and other watersports.

Theodore Roosevelt Lake

Dedication ceremonies of Roosevelt Dam (Arizona Territory), Col. Roosevelt speaking, March 18, 1911.

Lake Roosevelt, Arizona

Theodore Roosevelt Dam and the Roosevelt Lake it forms are considered perhaps the crowning achievements of SRP. With the initial funds raised by the association in 1903, an ambitious project was begun several miles east of Phoenix in the Tonto Valley, at the confluence of the Tonto Creek and the Salt River. When it was completed in 1911, Roosevelt Dam was the tallest masonry dam in the world at 280 feet (85 m). It was dedicated by U.S. President Theodore Roosevelt, for whom the dam and the reservoir are named.

In 1996, a massive expansion project aimed at increasing the capacity of the lake was finished. The dam was resurfaced with concrete and raised an additional 77 feet (23 m), which had the effect of increasing the lake's capacity by over 20%, and providing much needed flood control space on the Salt River. Shortly after completion, however, the area entered into a prolonged period of drought, and it would be some time before the new capacity was used, with the lake finally reaching historic levels of 90% capacity in early 2005.

With an at-capacity surface area of nearly 21,500 acres (87 km^2), Roosevelt is the largest lake that is wholly inside the state of Arizona. It can store 2,910,200 acre feet (3.59 km^3) of water at capacity.

Apache Lake

Horse Mesa Dam and Apache Lake

Apache Lake was formed by the construction of the Horse Mesa Dam, finished in 1927. Several miles downstream from Roosevelt, the dam stands 300 feet (90 m) high. The lake itself is considerably smaller than Roosevelt at only 2,600 acres (11 km^2) of surface area at full capacity, and can store 254,138 acre feet (313,475,000 m^3) of water.

Like the rest of the Salt River lakes downstream from Roosevelt, Apache Lake is long and narrow, filling the bottom of the canyon it resides in. It does have a hydroelectric generating station.

Canyon Lake

Canyon Lake, the third lake on the Salt River, is created by the Mormon Flat Dam. The dam was completed in 1925, being the second of the dams to be completed. The dam is named for a nearby geographical feature, a flat campground where Mormon pioneers from Utah would often stop on their journey to the Phoenix area. Downstream from Apache Lake, it is considerably smaller with only 950 acres (3.8 km^2) of surface area when full, holding 57,852 acre feet (71,359,000 m^3). Like the other Salt River dams, it is equipped with hydroelectric generators.

Saguaro Lake

Stewart Mountain Dam and Saguaro Lake

Saguaro Lake is formed by the Stewart Mountain Dam, downstream from Canyon Lake. Completed in 1930, it was the last of the reservoirs to be built on the Salt River. It is somewhat larger than Canyon but smaller than the others, having a surface area of 1,280 acres (5.18 km²) when full, holding 69,765 acre feet (86,054,000 m³). The dam is equipped with hydroelectric generators.

Verde River reservoirs and other dams

After completion of the four dams on the Salt River, SRP turned to the smaller Verde River for further expansion of the project. Like the reservoirs on the Salt, the Verde reservoirs are used for recreational purposes as well as water storage and flood control.

Bartlett Lake

The first of the lakes on the Verde River was created with the construction of the Bartlett Dam, finishing in 1939. At 308.5 feet (94 m) tall, the multiple-arch dam is lacking in hydroelectric generating capabilities, unlike most dams on the Salt River. Bartlett Lake, with 2,700 acres (11 km²) of surface area at capacity, is larger than all the Salt River reservoirs save Roosevelt. When full the lake can hold 178,186 acre-feet (219,789,000 m³) of water, or some 58 billion U.S. gallons.

Horseshoe Lake

Horseshoe Lake is formed by Horseshoe Dam and was finished in 1946, upstream from Lake Bartlett. Unlike the other dams built to this point, the construction was done by the Phelps Dodge Corporation as part of a water exchange agreement. In 1949, the city of Phoenix funded the construction of spillway gates for the dam in exchange for water rights for city users. Like Bartlett, this dam does not have hydroelectric generating capabilities. At 2,800 acres (11 km²) in surface area when full it is slightly larger than Bartlett but has a smaller total capacity, holding only 131,427 acre feet (162,113,000 m³) at maximum.

Blue Ridge Reservoir

Phelps Dodge, Inc., a large mining company in Arizona, constructed the Blue Ridge Dam in 1965 to help meet its water needs. A water exchange agreement penned three years earlier promised the facilities to SRP, and in 2005 SRP took possession of the dam and water production facilities. Located on the Mogollon Rim, Blue Ridge is not on the Salt or Verde rivers but is a part of the general watershed covered in the SRP area. The small lake has a storage capacity of only 15,000 acre feet (19,000,000 m³) of water.

Granite Reef Dam

The Granite Reef Diversion Dam, constructed near the confluence of the Salt and Verde rivers, does not actually hold back a reservoir but is used to divert water from those rivers into the system of canals feeding into the Phoenix area. It was actually the first of the dams constructed, finished in 1906 to replace the Arizona Dam, which had been washed away by floods the previous year.

Canal System

SRP operates several important canals that run in a network through much of the southern half of the Phoenix metropolitan area, helping distribute water from the Salt River system. Major canals operated by SRP are:
- Arizona Canal, 38.62 miles (62.15 km) long
- Grand Canal, 22.43 miles (36.10 km) long
- Consolidated Canal, 18.95 miles (30.50 km) long
- Eastern Canal, 14.73 miles (23.71 km) long
- Western Canal, 13.61 miles (21.90 km) long
- South Canal, 9.91 miles (15.95 km) long
- Tempe Canal, 9.76 miles (15.71 km) long
- New Crosscut Canal, 3.4 miles (5.5 km) long

SRP also operates a number of flood control canals throughout the Phoenix area.

Power generation

Besides the power generated at several of the dams along the Salt River, SRP owns or operates, in part, several power generating stations throughout the state:
- Agua Fria Generating Station
- Coronado Generating Station
- Craig Generating Station
- Desert Basin Generating Station
- Four Corners Generating Station
- Hayden Generating Station
- Kyrene Generating Station
- Mohave Generating Station
- Navajo Generating Station
- Palo Verde Nuclear Generating Station
- Santan Generating Station
- Arizona Falls

Source (edited): "http://en.wikipedia.org/wiki/Salt_River_Project"

Santee Cooper

Santee Cooper, also known officially from the 1930s as the **South Carolina Public Service Authority**, is South Carolina's state-owned electric and water utility that came into being during the New Deal as both a rural electrification and public works project that created two lakes and cleared large tracts of land while building hydro-electric dams and power plants. Its headquarters are located in Moncks Corner, South Carolina.

As one of the largest power providers in South Carolina, Santee Cooper directly serves more than 165,000 residential and commercial customers in Berkeley, Georgetown, and Horry counties. With a diverse fuel and energy supply of coal, nuclear, oil, gas, hydro and some renewable energy, Santee Cooper supplies power to the cities of Bamberg and Georgetown, 30 large industrial customers, and Charleston Air Force Base. Santee Cooper generates the power distributed by South Carolina's 20 electric cooperatives.

The people of South Carolina govern Santee Cooper through a board of directors appointed by the governor and approved by the state Senate. A board member represents each congressional district and each of the three counties where Santee Cooper serves retail customers directly; one board member has previous electric cooperative experience; and the chairman is appointed at-large.

Santee Cooper Lakes

The Santee Cooper Power and Navigation Project, constructed in 1939, improved navigation on and provided hydroelectric power from the Santee and Cooper rivers in South Carolina. With the creation of Lake Marion and Lake Moultrie, the project was intended to improve the health, recreation, and economy of the area. At the time, the Santee Cooper Project was the largest land-clearing project in U.S. history, with over 12,500 workers clearing over 177,000 acres (720 km) of swamp and forestland. 42 miles (68 km) of dams and dikes were constructed, including a 26-mile (42 km), 78-foot (24 m) tall earthen dike. The Pinopolis Dam included the hydroelectric station and navigation lock, the highest single-lift lock in the world. A 3,400-foot (1,000 m) spillway was built to control floodwaters, with 62 gates allowing overflow of excess water. In completing the largest earth-moving project in the nation's history, 42,000,000 cubic yards (32,000,000 m) of earth were moved and 3.1 million cubic yards of concrete were poured.

The $48.2 million project (55 percent federal loan, 45 percent federal grant) first generated electricity on Feb. 17, 1942. As transmission lines were built, power flowed to customers in Berkeley, Georgetown and Horry counties, and ultimately to electric cooperatives serving customers in 46 counties.

Biomass plant

A biomass plant to generate electricity for Santee Cooper will open in Newberry County, South Carolina in 2011
Source (edited): "http://en.wikipedia.org/wiki/Santee_Cooper"

Seattle City Light

Seattle City Light south service center, 1998.

Seattle City Light (SCL) is the public utility providing electrical power to Seattle, Washington and parts of its metropolitan area, including all of Shoreline and Lake Forest Park and parts of unincorporated King County, Burien, Normandy Park, Seatac, Renton, and Tukwila. About 740,000 residents are being served by Seattle City Light.

Seattle's electricity supply

For 2009, the fuel mix for Seattle City Light was approximately 91.2% hydroelectric, 4.4% nuclear, 2.3% wind, 1.4% coal, 0.6% natural gas, and 0.1% biomass and other sources. The utility owns and operates the Skagit River Hydroelectric Project, a series of three hydroelectric dams on the Skagit River in northern Washington State. The project supplies approximately 25 percent of Seattle's electric power. The utility also owns and operates the Boundary Hydroelectric Project on the Pend Oreille River which can provide up to approximately 50% of Seattle's electric power. The remaining power comes from a mix of sources, including long-term contracts with the Bonneville Power Administration (BPA). According to SCL, residential customers currently pay about 6 cents per kilowatt-hour of electricity. Seattle has the lowest residential and commercial electrical rates amongst comparably-sized cities in the United States.

History

Cover of Seattle City Light Yearbook, 1926

Public responsibility for electrical energy in Seattle dates to 1890 with creation of the Department of Lighting and Water Works. In 1902, Seattle voters passed a bond issue to develop hydroelectric power on the Cedar River (Washington) under the administration of the Water Department. Electricity from this development began to serve Seattle in 1905. A City Charter amendment in 1910 created the Lighting Department. Under the leadership of Superintendent James D. Ross, the department developed the Skagit River Hydroelectric Project, which began supplying power in 1924. Both public and private power were supplied to Seattle until 1951 when the City purchased the private electrical power supply operations, making the Lighting Department the sole supplier. The Boundary Project in northern Washington began operation in 1967 and currently supplies over half of City Light's power generation. Approximately ten percent of City Light's income comes from the sale of surplus energy to customers in the Northwest and Southwest. The current name of the agency was adopted in 1978 when the Department was reorganized.

Street Lights

On July 7, 2010 City Light began installing the first of 40,000 new LED street lights over the next five years.
Source (edited): "http://en.wikipedia.org/wiki/Seattle_City_Light"

Southern California Public Power Authority

The **Southern California Power Authority** is a joint powers authority, or a collective of 10 municipal utilities and one irrigation district. SCPPA was created in 1980 to help finance the acquisition of generation and transmission resources for its members. SCPPA is the 26th largest power company by net generation.
Source (edited): "http://en.wikipedia.org/wiki/Southern_California_Public_Power_Authority"

Tacoma Power

Tacoma Power is a public utility providing electrical power to Tacoma, Washington and the surrounding areas. Tacoma Power serves the cities of Tacoma, Fircrest, University Place, and Fife, and also provides service to parts of Steilacoom, Lakewood and unincorporated Pierce County. It is a division of the Tacoma Public Utilities and owns the Click! Network, developed by Steven Klein, Tacoma Power's former superintendent.

History

In 1884 Charles B. Wright was granted the exclusive right to create Tacoma's first power and water company, incorporating the Tacoma Light and Water Company. Wright's system drew water from Tule and Spanaway Lakes and Clover Creek. The water was transported to the city through a 10-mile wooden flume that emptied into an in-town reservoir. The flume was mostly uncovered and attracted thirsty cows and children in search of a good wading pool. This led to the spread of disease. Tacoma Power was created in 1893 when the citizens of Tacoma voted to buy the privately owned Tacoma Light & Water Company to ensure its safety and longevity.

Board of directors

Robert Casey, Chair
Peter Thein, Vice Chair
Laura Fox, Secretary
David Nelson, Member
Woodrow Jones, Member

Management team

William Gaines, Director of Utilities
Ted Coates, Tacoma Power Superintendent
Linda McCrea, Tacoma Water Superintendent
Dale King, Tacoma Rail Superintendent
Steve Hatcher, Customer Services Manager
Source (edited): "http://en.wikipedia.org/wiki/Tacoma_Power"

Taunton Municipal Lighting Plant

The **Taunton Municipal Lighting Plant** (TMLP) established in 1897, is a municipal electric utility within the city of Taunton, Massachusetts. Prior to 1897, the TMLP was the Taunton Electric Lighting Company, which lit Main Street/City Square area in 1892. It even made it possible to create the first electric car service [similar to trolleys] in the city in 1893. Today, the TMLP offer a wide arrange of services within the Greater Taunton Area, such as lighting services, an internet provider, and etc. It's a large and active municipal company in the region.
Source (edited): "http://en.wikipedia.org/wiki/Taunton_Municipal_Lighting_Plant"

Utah Municipal Power Agency

Utah Municipal Power Agency is a cooperative of cities in the State of Utah. The cooperative includes the cities and towns of Levan, Utah; Manti, Utah; Nephi, Utah; Provo, Utah; Salem, Utah; and Spanish Fork, Utah which each own their own electric utility systems. The electric cooperative allows each of the member cities to pool power generation, transmission, and other resources to make the purchase and sale of electrical power to their customers competitive and affordable.

Source (edited): "http://en.wikipedia.org/wiki/Utah_Municipal_Power_Agency"